# THE FRENCH MALAISE

# MALAISE

## Pyramid of CONTROL

BY **MARIELLE COEYTAUX**

*TRANSLATED FROM FRENCH*
*BY SHARON CALANDRA*

A VOICE YOURSELF PUBLICATION

# THE FRENCH MALAISE

## Pyramid of CONTROL

Printed in the U.S.A

ISBN 13-978-1477624814

ISBN 10-1477624813


For orders and information:
"BullyClear.com"

To "Mr. Hampe"
my high school teacher
who taught us the essence of Democracy:
*The right to think for ourselves.*

# TABLE OF CONTENTS

## PART I: DIAGNOSIS

# PART II: TRANSMISSION

# PART III: REMEDY

# ACKNOWLEDGEMENTS

I wish to acknowledge several people who actively contributed to the development of this book.

**Josette Santamaria:** for her precious help in writing this manuscript. Thanks to her knowledge of the French language, she carried out a rigorous reading of the text and offered many necessary revisions. Her encouragement and moral support were inspirational, without which I possibly would not have been able to bring this written work to publication.

**Berthe Davière:** whom I thank most particularly for her warm support during the various events that led me to this work.

**Dr. Claude Steiner** and **Rémy Filliozat:** two distinguished Transactional Analysists, who gave me the intellectual tools for comprehending the Belief System described in this book. Rémy Filliozat, trainer and psychotherapist, co-founded the School of Holistic Health in Paris (SA-MA-SA)[1]. Dr. Claude Steiner, clinical psychologist, co-founded "Transactional Analysis" and also created an international movement for teaching Emotional Literacy[2] (tools to develop openheartedness and cooperation). These two amazing teachers – one being French and the other Californian – have in common a great compassion for the human race and a deep concern for its wellbeing. Their many years of clinical experience have lead them both to a profound understanding of the human being, which they generously share with all those who care to learn. Their professional tools and personal insights greatly enlightened me, in my search to unravel the complex **relationship between the individual and his/her social context** (which is the main subject of the book). Their intellectual input was particularly enlightening in the association

---

[1]    http://conseils.en.sante.free.fr

[2]    http://www.claudesteiner.com/

they make between oppression / repression / suppression (of emotions) / depression.

**Dr. Anne Kohlhaas-Reith**[3]: an accomplished and worldly renowned Transactional Analyst, who is also my supervisor and professional mentor in Emotional Literacy. Anne is a woman of deep intelligence (both in the mind and heart), and her support—so generously offered with great kindness and authenticity—has opened up horizons to me that she cannot even imagine.

And **my four wonderful daughters:** who have continually motivated my search for greater understanding. Through them – beginning with their arrival into this world (conception and birth) – I learned that a child does not "belong" to his or her parents. *The child is (and needs to remain) the principle author of his/her own life.* He/she has an internal engine that we, as parents, can only encourage or obstruct.

Herein lays the result of my research—motivated by my love for my children, *and for all the children of this world*— recorded for you in this book.

Marielle Coeytaux

---

3    http://www.ta-kohlhaas-reith.de/

# PREFACE
by Claude Steiner

Reading Marielle Coeytaux's *"The French Malaise"*, I was very impressed by her elaborate historical and linguistic analysis of the influence of patriarchy on French and Western culture. Here I will comment on a central theme of the book: the global battle between patriarchy and democracy.

After millennia of domination by patriarchy, a global system that exploits and squelches people's power, individuality and free choice, we are entering a new era of huge democratic possibilities. The scheme that has eroded and slowed down people's potential is the patriarchal system of domination, which exploits most people for the benefit of a few powerful men and their chosen descendants, while leaving the rest to struggle merely to survive. The system that is now displacing this scheme that so undermines the collective potential of humanity is democracy, based on the principle that everyone is born with equal rights under the law, and should have equal access to the freedom to develop their full potential, awareness, spontaneity and intimacy.

The patriarchal system —elaborately analyzed by Coeytaux— is the logical, civilized extension of the genetically innate territorial and hierarchical nature of primates. Male supremacy among apes quite naturally evolved into a human system in which old powerful men ruled society with the help of their appointed male and female lieutenants. The system of patriarchy has ruled humanity without interruption from the dawn of history. The steady, albeit lurching, advance of democracy, which arguably started in the Greek City of Athens 500BC, is a reaction against the oppressive, ancient regime of patriarchy and its system of hierarchies and domination as culture evolves away from simian, ancestral survival patterns. In the 2500 years since its first appearance, democracy and patriarchy have been engaged in a titanic struggle, punctuated by dramatic, forward-moving democratic developments. The struggle goes on at many levels; the mechanisms of patriarchal oppression are complex. Some are overt such as land inheritance and ownership laws, the Inquisition's torture and burnings, professional guilds, unequal pay, voting right restrictions and on and on; the laws protecting the patriarchy are endless. Other mechanisms of oppression are subtle and imbedded in the culture; attitudinal, conversational and most importantly as elaborated by Coeytaux, linguistic.

The development of Christianity was a crucial step in the evolution away from patriarchy. The patriarchs of Jewish society viciously attacked Christ for his message of love and equality before God for the poor and downtrodden, ultimately crucifying him. Later, the patriarchs of the Christian Church criminally corrupted his message. Nevertheless, it was enough to sow the seeds of a more humane, democratic world view. The French and American revolutions, as Coeytaux points out, the emancipation of the American slaves, the various waves of feminism, the civil rights movement in the US, were important new expressions of the democratic impulse, and have helped to spread these ideas around the world.

The democratic struggle against patriarchy is at a crucial moment in history. Democracy was dealt a blow by George W. Bush's ham-fisted attempt to forcibly "spread democracy" to the Middle East.

Democracy is based on two principles: Freedom and Equality, both contradictory to patriarchal principles, which are based on hierarchies, and, if necessary, violent domination. In her last section of the book—Remedy—Coeytaux offers a valuable analysis of the freedom promoting elements in modern society.
This is a helpful and informative book for anyone who is interested in a detailed analysis of the extraordinary significance of patriarchy and democracy in contemporary society.

# FORWARD

This book is not a criticism of the French people. It is critical analysis of the *system* that governs France and that makes the French people suffer.

I originally wrote the book in French with the intention of helping my people understand our national malaise and find the remedy. Today, I am publishing these writings in English because the "virus" that causes our malaise knows no geographical boundary. It is prevalent throughout the world (in a more or less active mode), and inflicts its harmful consequences wherever it prevails. It is thus of universal concern.

May this book offer some enlightenment... *for the betterment of all people.*

Marielle Coeytaux

## I. OUR LANGUAGE DRIVES A FALSE BELIEF

Research conducted in Neuro-Linguistic Programming (NLP) has now verified that our maternal language (primary language used during early childhood) structures our thoughts. It drives our logical reasoning, concepts and symbols. People who are multi-lingual also know that each language has its own grammar, structures and ideas. Hence, how we think is significantly programmed by our maternal language. We are formed and deformed by it. Being aware of this offers the opportunity to free ourselves of the ideas that disserve us and our loved ones.

Languages transport beliefs. Although we are not aware of the beliefs they carry, they actively influence our thoughts and actions, sometimes leading us in directions we would rather not venture.

Our French language is primarily a Latin language. As such, it carries the beliefs of the Latin culture. An error of scientific nature, made very early in the evolution of mankind, progressively led our Latin civilization to a "false belief" that is still deeply embedded in our Latin-rooted language. Via our language, this unhealthy belief continues to influence our relationships, thwarting them to the point of making them dysfunctional. It engendered an abstract concept—entirely fabricated by the human mind—that legitimizes the use of power plays and causes interpersonal violence. Artificial and illusionary, it warps the natural laws of balance and reciprocity, locking people into relationships of dependency. By preventing them from achieving full maturity (i.e. taking complete charge of their lives and full possession of their human potential), it acts as an obstacle to personal growth and autonomy. By counteracting the natural law of reciprocity, it hinders the development of empathy and compassion – qualities so greatly needed in our world today. Most seriously, it sets the foundations for dictatorship, slavery and servitude.

As a French speaking nation, we—unknowingly—continue to practice and perpetuate this dangerous false belief. And in doing so, we lay the ground work for our own national malaise (gender and racial discrimination, domestic violence, social injustice, massive and expensive assistance programs, ever-recurring strikes, increasing tensions between social classes….).

It must be said (and emphasized!) that France does not hold the monopoly to this false belief; it is common to all patriarchal cultures. France does, however, have the misfortune of having it <u>structurally</u> embedded in all its institutions (political, religious and family).

## A.    THE FALSE BELIEF

The specific false belief that this book addresses is: that certain categories of humans are **intrinsically superior** to others and as such, are allowed to (and expected to) control those whom they believe "**intrinsically inferior**". In the name of their "superiority", they think for others, boss them around, tell them what to do, and punish those who don't obey. They rule *over* others; they set the rules of behavior for all those "under" them. What they say goes - **their will is the law.** They are assigned the mission of thinking for others, of dictating what others should do or not do, and power-playing them into compliance. Thus, in the name of their supposed "intrinsic superiority", they deny others the right to think and decide for themselves.

This concept of **Supremacy = Right to Dominate** (i.e. *Might is Right*) is explicitly expressed in the French term *'autorité'*, which the official French Dictionary (*Le Petit Robert*) defines as:

> "AUTORITE    1. Right to command, power (recognized or not) to impose obedience. = command, domination, force, power, sovereignty. Supreme authority, authority of the sovereign, of the head of State, authority of the superior over his subordinates, of the leader over his soldiers (= hierarchy). Paternal, parental authority. Authority of the guardian over the minor (= supervision). Legitimate, established authority; usurped illegal. Absolute authority, despotic, dictatorial, unlimited, uncontrolled, etc…"
>
> *Le Petit Robert*, edition 1996

The French word *autorité* (authority) derives from the Latin word *auctor* (*author* or *source* in English). As the etymology of the word reveals, this Latin concept associates authority with authorship. It grants to certain categories of individuals the right to take authorship of other people's lives, by taking command of their actions, ordering them around and forcing them into compliance. They treat others as their subjects, their personal soldiers, whom they will order around and use to fight their personal battles (thus satisfying their own personal needs, wishes, dreams and desires).

This type of Law and Order (that grants full power to a few *over* others) requires forceful and abusive tactics; because to force someone into compliance, there is no other way than to bully them into it or to bribe them. Bullying and Bribery are thus <u>necessary</u> to the works.  It is through the use of forceful and threatening tactics that an authority figure forces others to *"Do what I say"*.

This is the logic of servitude and violence: when a few individuals, who think themselves "superior" and thus "entitled", make themselves the authors of other people's lives through means of force and intimidation.

This concept of **HIERARCHY** (*the ruling of the 'superiors' over 'inferiors'*) strangely satisfies man's fantastical desire for absolute power. By placing some people 'on top' to control *over* those designated as 'below', it perverts the natural and healthy sense of authority, which is not based on status, but on competence.

### B.  The Genesis: An Error "In the Beginning..."

The Latin concept of authority, based on hierarchy (power granted by status rather than by competence), finds its roots in the beginning of times, when mankind understood very little of the laws of Nature. In the earlier millenniums of human development, people were subjected to matters of life and death with very little comprehension of the natural laws that governed their lives. They were subjected to serious weather conditions (without understanding them), to the laws of procreation (without understanding them), the laws of emotions and human relationships (without understanding them), etc...

Since human beings naturally fear what they don't understand (this seems to be a universal trait), the various human ethnic groups around the world called upon 'devins' (a French word that literally means 'guessers', and translates as 'soothsayers') to explain the mysteries of life. To reassure their people, these *devins/guessers* sought to explain natural events that occurred by linking them to human behavior. For example, natural catastrophes were explained as being the expression of the Gods' anger towards man. Thus, it was believed that man could appease God's anger by being "good": if man changed his behavior, natural catastrophes and their destructive consequences could be avoided. This logic reassured the people, for it gave them explanations to events they didn't understand (which is always reassuring) and it gave them the illusion that they had some kind of power over the laws of Nature: if they obeyed the *devins* and followed the *"Divine Will"*, they'd avoid triggering God's anger and would thus avoid death-threatening events.

Because survival (avoiding death) is always the bottom line for living beings, the people went along with the rules of the religious *devins/guessers*. And so it went on for several millenniums to follow: the *devins* - with their threatening tactics - reigned over the land... unopposed.

## 1) FEMALE DEITIES VENERATED IN PRIMITIVE RELIGION

The major issues that religious authorities (*guessers*) dealt with revolved around Life and Death. *What is Life? How did we get here? Where did we come from? What is our purpose in life? Where do we go after we die?* ... Creation and procreation were of the greatest concern, because they were complete mysteries to man.

Before the Neolithic Revolution (which began in Mesopotamia, around 10,000 BC), man had absolutely no understanding of the reproductive system. It was completely ignored that sex and pregnancy were in any way related. The people didn't perceive the link between cause and effect. They thought that life was a mysterious gift granted to women by some magical effect. They would see women's bellies grow (for no apparent reason), from which newborns would emerge many moons later. No association was made to the sexual act that had taken place several months before. The concept of "father" was nonexistent. It appeared that mothers engendered their offspring independently of the male gender. Women were thus regarded as Givers-of-Life and were respected and venerated as such. They enjoyed the status of **Procreators**.

The planet Earth – who provided food for all the living creatures – was associated to fertility and thus to motherhood. She was thus referred to as "Mother Earth". She too was respected and venerated.

As the text below shows, primitive religion centered on the theme of LIFE, venerating female deities and gods of fertility:

"Interest in LIFE took two complementary directions:
a.    **The Refusal to Die**
      Since the beginnings of religion…, man has wanted to believe that the death of a loved one wasn't final … This belief gave rise to several systems ranging from reincarnation to the belief in a kingdom of the dead, where ancestors existed, and whose lives had to be sustained through offerings and sacrifices (the ancestral cult)…
b.    **Veneration of Life Forces**
These forces are numerous, and each culture has its own particularities. Firstly: Procreation. Having children allows the tribe to continue living on earth and allows parents to live in the afterlife through the children's sacrifices. For a long time, interest in procreation benefited the status of women because it was she who procreated. Time was needed for man to understand the role he played in procreation. For a long time, it was believed that woman gave life herself, or in relation to the stars, the rain, the sea … "
      Cf. *Le Sentiment Religieux Primitif* by Gilbert Carayon, Evreux 1996

But human understanding of the laws of nature evolved. With time, scientific discoveries were made at all levels, offering better awareness of the laws of nature. An astonishing and revolutionary discovery was made at one point in the science of reproduction. We don't know the precise time of this discovery, but it clearly accompanied the Neolithic Revolution - a serious turning point in the evolution of human civilization. It was the era when man began understanding reproduction, making observations of cause-and-effect in the area of sexual activity in plants and animals. This new knowledge triggered the agricultural revolution, which brought on a wide-scale transition in human organizations, moving mankind from a lifestyle of hunting and gathering to agriculture and settlement.

Along with this knowledge of animal and plant reproduction came a simplified understanding of human reproduction. Man began to see the link of cause-and-effect between birthing and the sexual act that had taken place nine months earlier.

This discovery presented an astonishing revelation: the realization that man (the male) played an active role in human procreation. It was finally discovered that the child had a **father**! It was an extraordinary and crucial discovery in regards to family structure and child rearing. It gave the fathers recognition for their previously unacknowledged power in procreation. With that recognition, came sense of duty for the child's up-bringing.

But this awesome discovery was coupled with a terrible mistake that would prove to be tragic for millenniums to come. Because the discovery was incomplete, it would prove to be disastrous for the female gender: instead of improving the women's condition (providing mothers with the paternal help they needed to nurture the child to adulthood), it stripped them of their powers in almost all areas of human activity.

What exactly is this **mistake** that so disempowered the female gender? It was a *mis*-take on man's perception of reality (as explained here below):

The discovery of fatherhood shifted the power of procreation from women to men. It now granted sole power of reproduction to the man (the male). For it was now believed that the seed of life was produced (fully conceived) in the testicles of the male, leaving the female to being nothing more that the receptacle in which that seed would grow. The mother's contribution in providing and transmitting genes to her children was completely ignored (unknown), thus neglected and discounted.

> Still today in France, we call the testicles "*Les bijoux de famille*", which literally means *the family jewelry.*
>
> This expression clearly reveals the active role that this error continues to play in our people's belief system, granting men the predominant role in transmitting the family genes and the *family treasure.*

This terrible mistake - terrible in its consequences - can be explained by the lack of scientific means of the times. Without the technical equipment we have today, observations were restricted to what was actually visible to the naked eye. Regarding human reproduction, only the male reproductive organs were visible. The female's reproductive organs, hidden within her, were invisible to the naked eye. So it was believed that life, in the form of a seed, was created/generated/produced in the male genitals and then transmitted (through intercourse) to the female, where it would then grow; like a seed planted in the earth to germinate... The mother's true contribution – her actual 50% of transmitted genes, provided by her ovum and produced in her ovaries – thus remained completely absent from the equation.

This misunderstanding of human reproduction will justify neglect and abuse of women for thousands of years to follow. By designating the father as *sole* genitor, he was believed to be the **provider,** the **source** ('*auctor*' in Latin) of all future generations. In short, the survival of the species would be assured by him. This gave man an intrinsic superiority over his female counterpart. This "supremacy" entitled him to special consideration. His will, whims and desires were henceforth to be satisfied by his wife and his children... in the name of the "Devine Will", in the name of the survival of the specie...

The woman, in all of this, would henceforth be considered nothing more than a receptacle in which life (supposedly provided by the father) was to be deposited, via sexual intercourse. She was now viewed a simple object ...and would be treated as such. From here on, woman would have the moral obligation (religiously sustained) to be subservient to her male counterpart's desires.

**And that is how women lost their natural power as equal partners in the most extraordinary and most important achievement in the survival of the human species: the Transmission of LIFE.**


*2)      GOD BECOMES A FATHER FIGURE*

This scientific misconception (literally and figuratively speaking) will prove to have ENORMOUS consequences for everyone for millenniums to come:

**It directly affected religious beliefs.**
Theologies adjusted to this new (though erroneous) understanding of procreation. Representations of gods took on masculine faces. In many places, the male sexual organ became an object of veneration. Phallic symbols (obelisks, for example) were erected throughout the Fertile Crescent (region of Mesopotamia, where the Neolithic revolution first took place). Phallic symbols were erected as symbols of power. Power became associated to masculinity.

In the Near East, (near the Fertile Crescent) the many gods merged into one single, Unique God. This Unique God took on the title of "Father". He was represented as a domineering and *all powerful* masculine figure (as we can still see today in the Torah, the Bible, the Koran...). Throughout the sacred writings of the local religions, we see that God treat his people like the contemporary fathers treated their children at the time: with threats and punishments for those children who did not comply with his Will.

Mother Earth also finds herself affected by these theological changes. In the book of Genesis, in the Old Testament (a sacred book shared by many major religions – Jewish, Catholic, Orthodox, Protestant ...and others), we see the veneration of Mother Earth replaced by an order from God (now called *Father*) to dominate the earth. And sure enough, Mother Earth (and all of her resources) found herself equally subjected to man's whims and desires.

**It directly affected social and family interactions.**

As God took on a masculine figure, men seized upon religion, making it exclusively their business (by excluding women). Believing themselves endowed with a gender supremacy in the transmission of biological life, men went on to monopolize the power of transmission in all other domains of life, whether it was transmitting material possessions (of family inheritance) or intangible possessions (the family name, values, knowledge, profession, etc.). Women, meanwhile, found themselves evicted from all places where transmission occurred (schools, churches, and family inheritance) and were prohibited from participating in any of these domains. At best, they were authorized to act as *receivers*, but never as *transmitters*. Only man would be authorized to transmit knowledge. Only the father was permitted to transmit his name to the children. Only the children of male gender were to inherit the family's goods. As "Procreator and Giver of Life", the father would, from here on, consider himself "closer to God" than his female counterpart...

**It directly affected the women (and all the people with whom they interacted.**

Being excluded from the realm of knowledge (deprived of education), women's opinions no longer held weight against the opinions of educated men. The women thus found themselves less suited than their male partners in making good decisions.

22

Women had become dependent on men for knowledge. In this favorable position to decide for their female partners, men could now claim intellectual supremacy over women. They would now monopolize the right to speak up and to speak out. Women would henceforth be forced to remain *"à leur place"* (a very common French adage meaning *in their place*). And their place was one of **obedience and servitude**. This profound injustice would be their tragic fate for subsequent millenniums...

To add to the tragedy, this concept of **Hierarchy** created social and racial disparities. The religious justification of this domination of men over women subsequently legitimized all other dominations between adult (race, age, and class discrimination). For such is the law of nature: the type of relationship exercised by the parents (between themselves) legitimizes those types of relationship in the eyes of their children.


## C. THE FOUNDATIONS OF THIS FALSE BELIEF

*LAW OF STRONGEST (POWER TO THE MIGHTY)*

Access to knowledge having been made an exclusively male privilege, intelligence became an exclusively male attribute. Thus, intelligence became gender specific.

As men used their <u>physical</u> strength to compete for women (instinct of seduction), so did they with their <u>intellectual</u> strength. Knowledge became a source of power for rivalry. Thus, intelligence grew to be associated with **sexual power.** Men would seek to monopolize information or distort it to their advantage - whichever best served their purpose. The goal was to appear *the most* knowledgeable (in order to conquer). To establish their power once and for all (and avoid having it questioned), they created a hierarchal system of "superiors" over "inferiors".

Whoever appeared to be *the most intelligent* would assume Absolute Power over all the others. This logic of hierarchal status would be held with strategies of intimidation, strategies today known as BULLYING.

The clergy did not escape this logic. Initially endowed with an authority of divine knowledge, he was called the *Devin (guesser)*. But later on, he gains the title of *Sage* (the Wiseman - the One who Knows, and thus <u>advises</u>), as we see in Biblical passages. But the religious leaders gradually gain power and control over the people, and they do so by monopolizing the knowledge in their field. They higher their status by posing as *Seigneurs* (Lords: those who Know, Control and Command). In the Persian religion (where the Neolithic Revolution began), these religious leaders were called *Mages* (see exert below). Believed to have mysterious powers, they were regarded as being closer to God than the common, ordinary folk. Ceremoniously ordained, to certify them as belonging to the *Higher Order*, they were invested with a mission of divine authority (*mission sacerdotal* is the religious jargon in French for this concept). Their mission was to intercede between God and the "common mortals", protecting the latter from the wraths of the Heavens. As intermediaries between men and God, they were responsible for appeasing God (making sure that God's Will was satisfied so as to secure the safety of the people). Their duty was no longer to simply explain the laws of nature, but to control them - a superhuman endeavor! This, they carried out by presenting themselves as demigods, endowed with the power to make "rain or shine."

In the name of their superior knowledge of the Divine Will, the Clergy dictated Gods' Will, told people how to behave and what to do/not do. They would bully (intimidated) people into compliance and ostracize all individuals who didn't comply, (threatening them to be burn in hell, etc).

Clergymen thus went from the position of He-who-Knows-All to He-who-Commands-All. Obviously, living up to this superhuman endeavor of controlling Nature ("calming the angers of heaven") requires superhuman powers. So the priest had to appear powerful, very powerful, **MAGNUS**. To convince his flock of his superhuman/supernatural powers, he turned to magic, superstition and mystification.

---

"... *Magie* (Magic) comes from the Greek word *mageia*: witchcraft, art practiced by the *Mage*. The word *Mage* comes from *magos*, priest of the Persian religion.

In Latin, the root *mag-* expressed a notion of grandeur, leading to the words *magnus* (the great) and the superlative *maximus* (the greatest)... This root also gave forth to a comparative adverb 'more/greater than.' From *magis* came the title *magistère*, designating the person that had a status 'above/greater than' the others. *Magistère*, in French, became *maître* (master). Designating the person that commands, it engendered the title *magistratus*, from which comes the word *magistrat* in French (magistrates, in English)..."

Cf. "*Etymologies du Français*" de René Garrus, éd Bélin 1996

In French, we also find the words *magie* (magic), *magnifique* (magnificent), *magnitude* (magnitude), *major* (major), *maire* (mayor), *maître* (master), *mégalomane* (megalomania), *majuscule* (capital letter), *maximum* (maximum), etc.

---

The Romans pushed this megalomania to the point of attributing their religious authorities with the quality of **Infallibility**. Still today, the person at the top of the Roman Catholic Hierarchy – the Pope – is officially attributed the power of infallibility: he can never be mistaken. Thus, he cannot be questioned, and must be obeyed...

The entire Latin conception of law, order and authority (along with the authoritarian relationships that ensue) rests upon this one attribute— **the infallibility of authority figures.**

In order to control everything, the Magnus must not allow anything to escape him. He must demand that everyone submit to his will (with no space for discussion). He also demands that all initiatives first obtain his permission before being put into action. Believing himself responsible for all those entrusted to him[4], he attempts to control each person's movements and actions. Thus he places under his guardianship all those within his territory, dictating to them what they must do or not do (and punishing those who do not conform).

His word is the law and his inferiors are held to obedience and blind trust. By demanding authorization for every initiative taken, he makes himself the author of all actions that unfold upon his territory.

*Masters* must attempt to control the thoughts of those they claim responsibility for. They do this by discrediting any information that comes from another source than from them, and by distorting (to their advantage) the facts that they present. They are compelled to do this to maintain the illusion that they possess absolute knowledge, that they are always right, i.e. that they are **infallible**.

---

The word **PRESTIGE** comes from the Latin *praestigere*

"…which is nearly synonymous with *aveugler* (French for: 'to blind someone'). The Latin *praestigere* refers to 'throwing powder in the eyes'. The noun evolved into *praestigiae*, or 'tricks', and the synonym *praestigium*, 'the art of a charlatan, magician'. The word PRESTIGE that followed only took its positive meaning (attraction, glow) in the 13th century. Until then, it meant 'magic', 'art of illusion' (similar to *prestidigitaeur)…*"

Cf. "Les curiosités étymologiques" de René Garrus, éd Bélin 1996

---

4       "Entrusted" by whom???

The notion of absolute power, which leaves no room for discussion from the "subordinates", (take a close look at that word *"sub-ordinates"*...), still exists today. It has crossed several milleniums via religions, who endow their leaders with superior powers and qualify them as being "closer to God". In the name of their supposed intrinsic superiority, they force their will upon others, without having to worry about being held accountable for their bullying actions (since no one can question them). In numerous religions throughout the planet, people learn from the earliest age to follow the rules dictated by these designated authorities. The subordinates in these communities have no choice but to obey their superiors without criticism or discussion. They are obliged to do what they're told. They ask no questions nor do they request any explanation. They have been conditioned since childhood—through more or less painful physical and psychological strokes—to keep quiet, to not think for themselves (nor to act on their own). They must trust the superiors, who will do all the thinking and deciding. Their role, as subordinates, is simply to execute the orders "from above," from *Those-who-know-it-All and Must-be-Obeyed.*

### LYING: A NECESSARY STRATEGY

This dictatorial system, which requests that a few individuals dictate and impose their will upon others, continues to structure nearly all of our institutions in France (be they in politics, education, religion and/or family.)   Most all of our institutions are founded on hierarchical organizations, based on the principle of "authority from above". No matter if the "superior" is right or wrong, he still must be obeyed. He must not be questioned and he will not admit his faults. He still holds on to his pretense of infallibility.

Although times have changed and the attribution of superiority is no longer clearly a birthright (with the exception of gender discrimination), many of our country's "superiors" continue to act condescendingly toward their "subordinates". They monopolize information, steal the recognition for work well done, and refuse to be corrected or questioned to hide their mistakes. They continue to use methods of intimidation to get what they want, and consider themselves entitled to obedience in all areas, including sexual satisfaction.

Today's "superiors" are more commonly called *chefs*. They are the ones who, today, embody the authority to rule over others. What they say goes; their will is the law. They are designated by others above them ("even more superior") to regulate and control all those "below", who happen to find themselves within the given geographical area (a territory also designated by those "above"). There, they must Rule. They are expected to insure law and order and are held responsible if someone refuses to comply. This means ensuring that everyone marches in the direction dictated by the comrades from "above". This is done by sanctioning (punishing) all those who do not comply.

To be able to control everything that occurs "in their territory," they must present themselves as strong, *infallible* and invincible. They protect themselves from any question or discussion so as not to be corrected or proven wrong. They cannot acknowledge having made a mistake because admitting a mistake would mean betraying the confidence of their superiors, to whom they owe their own hierarchical status and power (and infallibility.) And it would also be very disappointing to their "inferiors," from whom they have demanded blind trust.

So...when a *chef* makes a mistake, what does he do? He denies it. He simply lies. He tries to hide the error and conceal it. And if someone sees the maneuver, he maneuvers to ostracize the unfortunate witness. This usually takes place with the aid of

28

other authorities of the institution, who share an interest in preserving the *chef*'s image, and who are eager to preserve the image of the institution that has granted them their power and their privileged status.

**Thus, lying is a survival strategy in the patriarchal system.** It is indispensable to maintaining the *collective illusion* of the infallibility of superiors.

Those who are considered "inferior"—today more commonly called *subordinates*—have no other choice than to obey the *chefs*. They are treated as infants: their opinion is never sought, and even if it is given, it is discounted. Their word has no weight.

---

The French word *enfant* ('Infant' in English) derives from the Latin word *in-fans* ('without speech')

Cf. Petit Robert French Dictionary, 1999

---

The subordinates are expected to carry out the orders (also referred to, in France, as "directives") of the *chef* without thinking or acting *"de leur propre chef"* (a common French expression that means 'of their own head').

---

The term *chef* literally means 'head' in French. The head is the organ of a body that has the function of thinking. It commands the other limbs (that act upon command, but cannot think). When someone has been appointed *chef* (head) of a group, he/she is granted the exclusive task of thinking for the group.

---

And when a *chef* commits an error, not much can be done to correct that error. For correcting a *chef*'s error is risky; it is directly acknowledging the fact that he is not infallible. Such an acknowledgement is rarely appreciated by anyone around, because it most commonly triggers some kind of reprisal (in the form of individual or collective punishment). So people choose to remain silent. And the error stands...

Thus evinced from the thinking process, the subordinates lend blind faith to the *Chef*, hoping that he will not err.

PYRAMIDAL STRUCTURE OF CONTROL

Infallibility is the keystone that secures hierarchies from top to bottom. Pyramidal structures are human organizations that place decision-making at the top, for issues that occur at all levels. The idea is that the one person at the top is intrinsically more intelligent than everyone else - about all things - and thus knows it all (for everyone) and will decide everything (for everyone). He dictates his wishes to the few below him, who then pass on the orders to those below them. In short, it's the top man who makes the decisions and the bottom folks who execute them, no questions asked.

From time to time, those at the bottom of the hierarchy—humiliated by this debilitating process—attempt to revolt and make themselves heard. But when this happens, those privileged by the system (those holding the reins of power) hasten to discredit the "agitators" by pushing a loud and strong reminder of the basic false belief that legitimizes their domination: *that certain human beings are invested with an intrinsic superiority that grants them innate knowledge, and that this grants them the right to dictate their will, **by force**.* Proclaiming themselves the Great Experts of Right and Wrong, they set out to force everyone to compliance and put the rebels "back on the right path"; which they do by isolating, invalidating and/or discrediting them.

It must be specified that many institutions around the world—and all of the world's armies—function this way (with a vertical and pyramidal hierarchy of commanders that demand obedience from those who are designated as "inferior"). This military system is clearly not a French invention. Nevertheless, what is specific to our country is that this militaristic way of functioning (with centralized power and a solid sense of hierarchy and obedience) extends far beyond our military institutions and operates in nearly all our  political, religious, social, family and professional institutions. And despite all of our historical attempts to free ourselves of it (see historical study further on), we have not yet succeeded.

# II. POWER PLAYS

This system of relationships, where some people act as Lords and Masters, is described in the Petit Robert French Dictionary as *"le fonctionnement relationnel feudal"* (*feudal relationship model*). It operates through obedience and submission, enforced by power plays. Power plays are coercive, bullying and/or manipulative strategies that are used to force people into doing things they wouldn't naturally choose to do. Since *obedience* is not a natural human inclination, it can only be obtained by force, by use of physical and/or psychological intimidation. The various strategies of intimidation are called power plays, as described below.

## A. Obedience and Submission

Obedience is a conditioned response, obtained by creating fear of reprisal. For this, methods of intimidation are used (threats of physical or psychological punishments). To obtain obedience, the superiors threaten to punish those who do not follow their will. And they do so with a clear conscious, because they are convinced that this is their duty: to ensure that everything runs well. They believe it is their obligation to force the "rebel" to regain the "right path" (which is none other than *their own* path). The expression "I will teach him a lesson" actually means "I will punish him". The punishments may be physical (inducing direct physical pain) and/or verbal (provoking psychological hurts, such as verbal insults that present the victim as idiotic, ugly, weak, crazy or sick). The belief that punishment is necessary to bring someone back to reason is so deeply integrated into Latin culture that Latin authorities will go so far as to call these intimidating methods 'sanctions' (from the Latin *sanctus*, or saint). Thus, in the Latin culture, the act of punishing someone (to hurt him/her) is an act of sanctification (leading him/her closer to God).

The French expression *"Qui aime bien, châtie bien"* (He, who loves well, punishes well) fits perfectly within this Latin *'culture de chef'*, which we have inherited.

This type of relationship (domination/submission)—which uses physical and/or psychological "whipping" strokes to keep the other person down (in a "one down" position, a position of "inferiority")—feeds into the entire vocabulary of the French language. According to the *Petit Robert Dictionary*, the notion of respect in Latin culture is always tainted with a notion of superiority and associated with induced fear (cf. definitions of the words: *veneration, homage, reverence, eminence, excellence, distingue* (distinguished), *dignitaire* (dignitary), *seigneur* (lord), *maître* (master), *chef* (boss).

## B. "THE CHEF IS ALWAYS RIGHT"

*Le chef a toujours raison* is a very common French expression (often spoken as a joke, but still stated). It literally means "The *chef* is always right."

Today, in France, someone who holds a position of authority is called a *chef*. The *chef* is the one who thinks for/ decides for /commands all others. The *chef* is the modern version of the feudal *Lord* and the *Master* in times of slavery. He possesses a given territory (physical and/or virtual) and he, alone, makes all the decisions for those who find themselves "on his turf." He decides what is good or bad for them, most often without consulting them directly, and uses strategies of intimidation to lead them in the direction he has chosen. His will upholds as Law over the entire territory, regardless of his competence in the matter. He demands "due respect" (which implies *obedience*). He is the only one authorized to take any initiatives in that area and will scrupulously protect the <u>exclusivity</u>

of this privilege.[5] All those who wish to take an initiative *on his domain*, must ask him for "authorization".

> The French expression *marcher sur les plates-bandes de quelqu'un* (to walk on someone's flowerbeds) appropriately illustrates this idea of 'stepping on someone's territory' when taking an initiative without prior 'authorization'.

Generally, the *chef* will try to intimidate or humiliate whoever fails to give him what he wants. Since his quality as "The Only Man Who Knows" defines his position, the simple act of questioning him poses a threat to his position. This is why anyone who contests the *chef's* word—even if the facts prove him to be objectively and visibly wrong—will be commanded to silence (by the *chef* himself or by others who need to protect the *chef's* image).

## C. THE "CRITICAL PARENT"

To ensure that *His Will* is carried out (*that his norm is maintained*), the *chef* will intimidate his interlocutors and demean those who dare to challenge him. He/she will do so by adopting an intimidating and condescending attitude: voice tone, gestures and words that reflect his or her "one up" position. Hence he/she will adopt an attitude of arrogance (a behavior well-described in Eric Berne's *Transactional Analysis*). He will act from his "Critical Parent" (which very appropriately translates to *Normative Parent* in French),[6] dictating *his norm* to the group, using words like "You

---

5     This has an eerie resemblance to the "exclusive territory" system of dominant male gorillas, who behave as if they owned the females that are on their territory.

6     The terms "Parent Ego State" and "Critical Parent" come from Transactional Analysis, a school of thought in psychology that offers interesting and highly effective tools for understanding human relationships. I am using this jargon here for my Transactional Analysis colleagues (who constitute a large percentage of my readers), to connect my work with that of Eric Berne's, the founder of Transactional Analysis.

have to," "you must," "you should," etc. He will impose obligations, principles and values he deems necessary to get his way and keep the dictatorial system working (with him on top).

I worked in France for several years with Transactional Analysts and I have observed that they have a harder time than other Transactional Analysts from other countries to integrate Eric Berne's major combat against the "Normative Parent." They argue that the Normative Parent is necessary and cannot be relinquished without sacrificing law and order. This they believe, because in their logic of "power to the Chef", NORM and LAW converge; they are one and the same: *it is the _norm_ of some that sets the _law_ over others.*

# III. THE RESPONSIBILITY OF PATRIARCHAL RELIGIONS

As previously described, this *chef*-system is founded on the principle that it is legitimate that some individuals impose themselves on others via strategies of intimidation, forcing them into obedience. It is most surprising to note that this system is driven by patriarchal religions, because the "law-of-the-mighty" is precisely what these religions spend much of their time and energy preaching <u>against</u>.

How do patriarchal religions enforce this *chef*-system? Recall that patriarchal religions, run exclusively by men, describe their God as masculine and thus justify their exclusion of women from their decision-making process. They impose themselves upon women, enforcing their male interpretations of the "Divine Law" by way of threats. This model of behavior, presented by the patriarchal churches, offers a troubling example to their male "laymen," who use it to justify their bullying behavior in family life. Then there are the Churches' exclusion of women in their decision-making process. The exclusions and the injustices exercised by the patriarchal churches are then propagated throughout the social contexts, where women are generally under-valued and subjected to masculine "directives."

---

In male-chauvinistic cultures (where patriarchal religions prevail), men state the laws and impose them on women. It is interesting to note that the female gender, in those cultures, is commonly called "the weaker sex" and the male gender is considered "the stronger sex." Is this not **explicitly legitimizing** the ruling of the "strong" over the "weak"…?

---

Considerable psychological damage is caused by this feudal logic of Unilateral and Vertical law, driven by the patriarchal churches. And this damage occurs first and foremost within families. In patriarchal families (those that practice a strictly masculine-structured religion), the father of the family is seen as being the *head of the family*. He imposes himself using threats and humiliation (physical and/or psychological) and reigns as master, authority over all those who live under his roof (his 'territory'). His wife and children are his property, obliged to fit into his plans, and to satisfy his desires and needs: as he wants, when he wants. Rarely can the issue of reciprocity be addressed in a couple of a patriarchal religion. *"Love thy neighbor as thyself"* is rendered impossible.

Currently in France, patriarchy in families is much more subtle than before. It even appears more like a matriarchy (i.e. household run by the mother). This, however, is only an illusion to the inexperienced eye, because closer examination reveals that this matriarchy, which I call 'patriarchal matriarchy', is simply a coordinated response to the patriarchal logic (subject developed in next chapter).

Nowadays, religion in France is far less prominent that it was. With the exception of Islam on the growing Islamic population in France, religion doesn't have much authority on the French. However, the imprint left by the Roman Catholic Church on our country – through its institutional structure, its language, its logic and especially through the examples it gives in the management of its internal relationships – remains huge. Many of the French people continue to function according to the Roman Catholic model. The French are not aware of this and can hardly be expected to be, since that is all they have experienced for over two millennia. But the fact is that the principles enforced by the Roman church on our country (its principles of *obedience, sacrifice, duty and obligation, submission to 'superiors,' infallibility*, etc.) continue to influence and disrupt daily relationships. No one can escape it fully. Couples, families, in-laws, siblings, teachers, students, civil servants, workers, etc. all live under hierarchal pressure, having to conform to directives imposed by those who hold "precedence" over them. Most everyone will abstain from expressing their free will for fear of "paying the price." They realize that the free spirits who defy the norms dictated by the familial, educational and/or religious 'authorities' will ultimately be discredited and alienated. They will be labeled and treated as:

- **"Abnormal/Crazy"** by the intellectuals 'authorities' of the dominant culture, who cannot comprehend how anyone in their 'right mind' can think or act differently than they themselves would (and therefore *should*).

- **"Irresponsible"** by family 'authorities', who get scared when they see another adult refuse submission (which *they* accepted, though would have preferred not to).

- **"Selfish/Damned"** by religious authorities, who cannot admit having one from their flock escape their realm of salvation Since they consider that all souls that stand on "their territory" are theirs to 'save', they will punish the independent souls for straying from the "Righteous Path" that they dictate. The punishment will be to ostracize the independent thinker, by falsely accusing him/her of selfishness and invalidating his/her intentions. The independent thinker is presented as a threat to the group, and treated as such (to be shunned to the point of being stripped in all regards).

The only people who can speak freely without too much risk of being ostracized are those who have already been acknowledged as 'superior' (by way of their big money, prestigious genealogical lineage or socially powerful profession).

# IV. HARMFUL CONSEQUENCES OF THIS SYSTEM

A social system based on hierarchical (dominant/ dominated) relationships is very unhealthy, for everyone. It produces numerous harmful side effects, listed here below:

## A. Psychological Effects

### 1. It prohibits the necessary expression of emotions

The first serious consequence is that emotions are repressed.

Indeed, this system does not allow the expression of **anger**, for it is experienced by all the 'subordinates' who have been deprived of the right to be the main author of their own lives. Allowing the expression of this anger would mean admitting to the legitimacy of this emotion (and thus, acknowledging the injustice of the system)

It will not acknowledge the **sadness** of all those who have been deprived of their freedom to think and the right to make their own choices. These people rarely find sympathetic ears to hear their complaints and share their burden. They will need to turn to professional listeners (psychologists) to find attentive ears. Interestingly enough, this listening process in psychology is called "therapy"... as if there were some kind of illness involved...

It cannot take into consideration the enormous amount of **fear** that it fosters:

- The fear of reprisal harbored by the "inferiors" when they don't satisfy the *chefs'* will.
- The fear that weighs heavily on the *chefs*, most of whom know very well, in the depths of their souls, that their supposed infallibility is only pretense, and that they

will never live up to the required level of perfection that is expected of them.

The emotions that can freely be expressed in this system based on obedience and submission to the hierarchy are those that feed the system: **pride** (in fulfilling one's duty), **shame** (for having failed) and **guilt** (of baring needs that conflict with the *chef's* desires). And possibly **joy** (in success), but only to a limited extent, because a *chef* usually doesn't appreciate it when someone other than himself succeeds. Most often, he will feel threatened and react punitively.

There is actually a French expression for this risky phenomenon: *Trop briller fait ombrage au chef*, which literally means, "Shining too brightly puts the boss in the shadow."

Emotions must thus be repressed. Expressing them directly is forbidden. However, they insinuate themselves through cynicism and mockery; two very common forms of expression in our French culture.

And is well proven by the science of holistic health (and taught by the SAMASA School of Holistic Health in Paris), pain and tension that cannot be expressed verbally will express itself through the body. Hence the appearance of many types of psychosomatic aches and pains. And contrary to the common belief, these aches and pains are real, they are *physically* painful:

- **Anger** and **Fear** secrete toxic elements in the blood and produces nervous tensions throughout the physical body, causing various pathologies (high blood pressure, ulcers, sexual anomalies, dermatitis, headaches, backaches, allergies, spasmophilia, insomnia, etc.).

- **Sadness** translates into muscular fatigue. This unexpressed sadness can lead to depression, to despair, and may even lead to suicide. Alcoholism and drug abuse serve the victims as means of "temporary relief".

**2.** It inhibits some individuals...

Within this system of highly centralized power and hierarchal relationships, many individuals find it impossible to fully exercise their ability/power to speak up and take initiatives. Being prevented from speaking up by those who monopolize the right to do so, the inhibited individuals develop "limiting beliefs" about themselves and foster inferiority complexes. These inhibitions can be quite obstructive and may require intensive therapeutic work to overcome.

**3.** ...and develops an illusion of absolute power in others

Those in the "superior spheres" of the hierarchical pyramid may get lost in an illusion of absolute power, and will encounter great difficulty in challenging that illusion as time goes by. Time will actually reinforce it. Those who believe themselves to be superior will think of themselves invincible and without limitations, and will defy all that gets in their way. The individuals particularly vulnerable to this phenomenon are those who were attributed a role of superiority/authority in their early childhood. Often it is the eldest child, who is made to believe that he/she "should know better" than his/her siblings. This designated status of "superiority" at the earliest age of growth creates and enforces a belief that the others aren't as smart as they are (since they, themselves, are the ones to supposedly "know better"). This, in turn, makes them feel responsible for all those around them. And as they grow up, they continue to act as if their peers were not capable of being responsible for themselves.

As adults, these individuals find it very challenging to engage in any self-questioning. Rather than admit their errors, faults and/or limitations – which would shatter the illusion of their infallibility – they find it easier to put the blame on others. This reflex (that conveniently avoids self-questioning) expresses itself in their language and directly affects their entourage. For example, they will say, "**You are** complicated!" rather than say "I don't understand you." They will say "**You are** worthless!" instead of saying "**I am** frustrated that I can't get what I want from you." Thus, rather than recognize their own limitations or faults (which they have, but cannot admit), they insult the person who confronts their limitations.

These insults are the primary source of inhibitions that drag down the dominated members of the system.

---

In French, the word POUVOIR means several things:
- As a noun, it means POWER
- As a verb, it means both **can** (capable of) and **may** (permission to)

Though these two notions—permission and capability—are expressed by the same verb, they are in effect two very distinct notions: there are many things one *can* do, but *may* not do (and vice versa). Not having separate words to differentiate these two separate ideas creates a serious ambiguity. Effectively, by combining permission and capacity in one single word, our language fosters serious confusion between the two notions. Our language leads us to believe that *capacity* and *permission* are, in reality, one-and-the-same thing. We are lead to believe that we are capable of doing only what we have permission to do, and we have permission to do only what we are capable of doing.

And the fact that only a few are "authorized" to do certain things implies that only those few are *capable* of doing them. Conversely, those "not authorized" to do something grow to believe that they are "not capable" of doing them.

---

## B. Socio-Political Effects (Behavioral responses)

### 1. It encourages dishonesty and hypocrisy

As noted above, in order to comply with the belief of infallibility, *Chefs* cannot admit their errors. So when a *Chef* commits an error, his reflex is to conceal it. And to do this, his simplest strategy is to deny it. Or if the error is too visible, he will admit that an error was made, but will transfer the responsibility onto someone else. This inflicts great injustice onto the unfortunate scapegoat, who will have to deal with all the consequences (including all the triggered emotions that the victim feels but has to suppress, such as fear, anger and/or sadness).

While <u>overt lying </u>is the *chef*'s strategy of choice to deal with his mistakes, <u>lying by omission</u> will be the *subordinate's* choice. This is because *subordinate* knows, in advance, that *chef* won't admit his mistake and that he'll most probably resort to his powers of intimidation to keep the truth under silence. So, to avoid being subjected to the *chef's* strokes of intimidation, the *subordinate* will choose to remain silent and do as he's told.

Dishonesty and hypocrisy thus result from the apprehension of getting into trouble, for both the *chef* and for the *subordinate.*

### 2. It teaches people not to speak up for themselves, but *for* others and *through* others

The example set by the "superiors," who allow themselves to speak in the name of others (most often without consulting them, nor informing them), legitimizes the fact that people speak and think for one another. Because of this, feelings and opinions and are not clearly differentiated from one person to another. It is unclear who is who, who thinks what and who feels what. So to navigate in this relational "fog," one must guess (assume and presume) what individuals really think or feel. One learns to "read" other people's minds, most often jumping to false conclusions and projecting their own emotions and thought processes. Psychological projections prove to be abundant and relationships get confusing. One easily gets lost in the confusion. Confusion leads to misunderstandings and misunderstandings lead to conflicts. Conflicts of this sort are traumatic and can lead to great tragedies (murder, suicide...).

### 3. It perverts communication

Unable to freely express their emotions (the system's first consequence), people feel obligated to speak in coded form, with "hidden messages." To express one thing, the speaker will say another.

For example: *"Great!"* (said with a sarcastic tone) will in fact mean *"This is worthless!"* Or: *"Hey, your hair looks nice today!"* said in a certain tone of voice can actually mean *"Your hair really looks bad today!"* This phenomenon is well described in Transactional Analysis.

This coded language greatly complicates communication. For, if the *spoken* words do not really mean what they say, then what do they mean?! In such a context, where what is verbalized actually means something else (and sometimes the exact opposite!), a person who speaks frankly can get into unexpected trouble. Making a simple compliment can prove to be risky, since a given compliment can be turned into a direct insult (if interpreted by the receiver to mean its contrary). The misunderstandings provoked by such distorted communication are endless!

## 4. It poses obstacles to mutual assistance

In a patriarchal context, *requests* are actually *orders* (demands that cannot be refused without suffering punishment). This linguistic confusion—between a *request* and an *order*—creates serious ambiguity in people's minds. For when a *true request* is expressed (one that actually allows for refusal, without punitive consequences), it will usually be understood as an *order*.

Such a context does not leave much leeway for expressing true requests (especially if it's a request for help). Knowing in advance that people feel **obligated** to respond to all requests—even if they don't really have the means (or desire) to do so—it is difficult to ask for help. So, out of empathy for our loved ones—so as not to overload or embarrass them—we learn not to ask for favors. We just try to manage... on our own, alone.

Another reason for not expressing requests in patriarchal cultures is that they very often trigger aggressive, rebellious responses. Though a defensive reaction can be a positive, adapted response to a *dictatorial order,* it certainly is *not* an adapted response to a *request*. Some people—who are very rebellious to *orders* and who don't distinguish a *request* from an order—will respond aggressively to even the most neutral *request*. For example, if we were to ask her *"What time is it?"* in a slightly worried tone of voice (because we're a bit worried about being late), we may provoke in her a surprisingly aggressive reaction. The reason for this aggressive response is that she has interpreted our request as being some kind of *disguised parental order* (*"It's late! You should go home!"* for example). Our question was requesting purely factual information, but was heavily thwarted by her misinterpretation of it (partially induced by our worried tone of voice that she interpreted as anger... against her). This response may surprise us and scare us by its accusing tone. It may then lead us to respond in an equally defensive tone, which may trigger a yet more angered response...

Making false assumptions, jumping to conclusions and misinterpreting the speaker's motivations are all common causes for inappropriate responses.

But the primary reason why requests are not easily expressed in a patriarchal culture is that they express a *need*. Affirming a need can prove to be a risky affair. It suggests that the "superior" did not fulfill his duty of meeting all the needs in "his territory". He will get angry and scared, which will put the "inferior" at risk of being subjected to additional negative strokes.

### 5. It discourage gestures of love

In this context, where the principles of duty and obligation rule, each person's role (actions) is well-defined by the cultural authorities. These well-defined roles actually obstruct the free flow of expressions of love. For in effect, an act of love (a gift or a kindness) will not produce joy, but will instead induce conflict. The reason for this is that most gifts are pre-assigned to a specific role, locking them into one of two categories.

Either the gesture is

- already *expected* of us, in the role assigned to us by the pyramidal scheme (for example, a meal prepared by a woman for her husband)

Or

- it is *not expected* of us in our assigned role (such as a woman taking her husband out to a restaurant).

In both of these examples, a woman shows her love to her husband by offering him a nice dinner. However, in neither of these cases will her gesture of love be acknowledged as such: 1) in the first case her gesture will be considered a normal thing (since it's her "duty" to cook dinner), 2) in the second case, the gesture will be taken as an <u>insult</u>, because it will place him as the receiver (the "one-down" position in this culture), putting her in the position of being the 'provider' (a privilege exclusively reserved to him). Thus, in both cases, the original intention is lost. Instead of generating or fostering feelings of *love,* it will simply have added tension to the relationship.

So, in order to avoid "offending" their loved ones, most people carefully remain in their clearly defined roles, only to venture in acts of kindness that lie within their pre-determined and officially authorized specified domains. Acts of love are thus constrained to the realm of the expected (mandated), where they are not perceived as anything other than *"just the normal scheme of things".* Affectionate ties slowly fade into insipid, odorless and colorless relationships, tarnished by conventions...

**6.** <u>It encourages manipulative strategies and hidden</u> <u>agendas</u>

When people have learned to <u>not</u> speak for themselves, but rather to count on others to express their needs and desires, communication is distorted and relationships get complicated.

- For example: a mother who needs help, but can't admit it, will say to her child "Your father wants you to ...." Thus, the mother uses a third party (the father, in this example) to get what she needs without requesting it on her own behalf. The problem is that, in doing so, she places the responsibility of the command onto the father, who will have to deal with ensuing consequences.

- Another example of how one uses a third person to achieve one's personal goal: A father says to his son: "Your mother won't join us, she's too tired" (when in reality, the mother is neither tired nor has she even been informed of the event in question). This is actually a roundabout way to say "I want to do this alone with you." Such lies frequently occur in patriarchal families, where adults hide behind each other to say what they cannot express directly.

This kind of communication is very disturbing for a child because it distorts reality. When reality is thus perverted (disguised), the child gets lost and confused. The important distinction a child needs to make in order to gain personal autonomy is "you are you and I am me". But this distinction cannot be made because *confusion* keeps everyone *"fused"* together (*"con-fused"* comes from the Latin *"merged with"*). Such relationships are called 'fusionnal relationships'.

Another example of perverted communication: guilt tripping someone in order to get him/her to do something that he/she does not want to do, and involving an involuntary third party.

- For example *"Aren't you ashamed of hurting your mother by doing this?!"* when in fact the mother has no pain, and is completely unaware that she is being used to make the child feel guilty. Result: the child has it out for his mother (for reasons independent of her and completely unknown to her).

Perverted communication presents itself in a myriad of forms, always distorting the truth in some way or another to benefit the one who is doing the distorting. The *psychological games* described by Eric Berne (founder of Transactional Analysis) in his book *Games People Play* find their source in such a context, where speaking frankly or openly about a problem is prohibited.

### 7. It encourages rape and abuse

In this system, where might makes right, the will of the strongest is imposed upon the weak,[7] leaving the door wide open to violence – particularly violence waged against women. Indeed, if the "superior's" <u>desire</u> is sufficient to legitimize his act, and if men are considered "superior" to women, the high prevalence of rape in patriarchal societies is perfectly logical.

The victims of rape or mistreatment will submit to abusive acts with little defense, for they know they cannot oppose the authorities. The victims have been conditioned, from the earliest age, to submit to the will of their "superiors." Though it hurts terribly and seems atrocious, the victims will remain silent. And so will everyone around, for one must not speak up on subjects that are "shameful". They remain taboo, for they would stain the *chef*'s image and cause him to retaliate: the greater the stain, the greater the retaliation. Thus, abominable acts of abuse remain officially undetected and unpunished. Violence is thus kept in a closed circuit, feeding on silence and perpetuating itself.

### 8. It imposes the rule of silence

This authoritarian system, that grants all power to one single individual in a defined territory, grants the freedom to speak/think to only one person: the *Chef*. The others must remain silent. People remain silent because they all know that whoever dares speak up will be punished. Thus, silence is kept by the reign of fear. Anyone daring to speak up about any injustice committed will be reprimanded. Speaking out foreshadows a conflict and possibly violence.

In this system, there is only one valid perspective to view the world, and it is the *Chef*'s. Different perspectives cannot be expressed. Thinking differently than Him would challenge his identity as "He who Knows All" (and immediately trigger a defensive reaction on his part). As a result, everyone keeps quiet. Children are told, *Mange ta soupe et tais-toi* ("Eat your soup and

---

7      The criteria distinguishing the strong from the weak is always set by those in power, which is how the system perpetuates itself.

shut up"), and women are made to understand *Sois belle et tais-toi* ("Be beautiful and shut up)."

Furthermore, since the *Chef* is infallible, any person "under his authority" must also appear to have no faults. This is embedded in the logic, since admitting to a problem in a given area is indirectly accusing the *Chef* of failing his duty (which is to control his sector). So, in order to uphold the *Chef*'s good image, everyone maintains an image of perfection, pretending that there is no problem, that "everything is rolling along" smoothly.

Thus, in patriarchal cultures, people learn to conceal their difficulties. They do not speak openly about their problems so as to avoid giving displeasure/discomfort (shame) to the one who is designated as the *Responsable* (another French word for "*Chef*"). And since the defense mechanism of the *Responsables* is to strike when they stand corrected (hurling physical and/or psychological blows to the person who is informing them, rather than simply acknowledging the existing problem), the best strategy to remain safe is to pretend that everything is going smoothly. Thus rules the Law of Silence.

### 9. It leads to familial matriarchy

This system of unilateral law—where it is considered legitimate (even necessary) that one single person make the law (be the law) over the others—poses yet another unhealthy side effect: matriarchy.

Matriarchy, as it presents itself in this context, is a direct sub-product of patriarchy. Patriarchy embraces the logic of "only one captain on board". And since traditional patriarchy considers men better adapted to handle external affairs (being "intrinsically superior in intelligence"), he is expected to fully devote himself to external affairs. The woman is consequently assigned to the home, where she must fully devote herself, single-handedly, to the internal affairs (this answers the masculine principle of "only one captain on board"). There, in the household (which her husband designates as "her territory"), she is expected to do everything, handle everything, and control everything that happens. She is given the title of *'Maitresse de maison'* ('Master of the house') and is expected to assume complete parental responsibility, alone. And so she will, in accordance with the concept of "authority" that was taught to her by her cultural references (imposed on her, as a child). As the governor of the household, she may act as an "enlightened despot", or she may proceed as an authoritarian oppressor (power playing to obtain what she wants). But however she plays the role, she will be acting as dictator, transmitting the fundamental principle of patriarchy to her children: that it is legitimate for one individual to unilaterally impose his/her will onto everyone else.

Patriarchal matriarchy is very damaging for all members of the cellular family.

> In families where one authoritarian parent imposes his/her choices upon the children, refusing all discussion or any questioning (which is characteristic of an authoritarian figure), <u>the children</u>:
>
> - inherit their parents' battles, unconscious drives, concealed faults and weaknesses.
> - quickly understand that adulthood means "being in a position of always being right and not having to take others into consideration". Because growing up means becoming authorized to impose one's will on others, using physical or psychological strokes if necessary.
> - find themselves deprived of a secure home, where responsibilities are truly shared, where mutual and

reciprocal satisfaction and questioning are encouraged.

Furthermore, in French families, the law of the strongest is *legitimized* by the fact that the eldest child is explicitly granted the right to rule over his or her younger brothers and sisters. This is a traditional French birth right, known as *"le droit d'ainesse"* (which literally means "the right of the eldest"). *The law of the strongest* appears here in its most unrefined state, setting the premises to all the patriarchal beliefs, with their most pernicious consequences: the eldest will adopt the authoritarian behaviors that he or she witnessed from his/her parents (or other parental figures), and the younger siblings will serve as "privileged outlets" for his/her anxieties and frustrations. In the position being held "responsible" for his/her younger siblings, he/she will have to force them into "obedience" by way of intimidation (threats of physical or psychological punishment, depending on his/her available "forces"). And he/she will include power plays to satisfy his/her personal "drives." Children—thus abandoned to this "law of the jungle"—can be very hard on each other, wounding each other in ways that can remain strongly imprinted in their hearts and/or bodies. These deeply imbedded scars can provoke consequent family conflicts that may prove to be very difficult to resolve without professional help.

The mothers, held "solely responsible" within the family sphere, are usually overwhelmed by all the tasks that fall upon their shoulders. They are held responsible for everything and everyone and must turn themselves inside out to hold everything together. And they must do so with a smile, giving the impression that "everything is running" perfectly. As *"the parental authority"*, they cannot express their suffering or difficulties, needing to appear perfect and without any faults. Deprived of recognition and of personal satisfaction in this task, they turn to religious authorities, who promise them better treatment in an "after-life." Religion provides them with hope of compensation "from Heaven" if they carry the burdens inflicted upon them without complaining, "*en paix*" as they say in French (expression that literally means "in peace," but subtly means "without disturbing *our* peace"). Thus, the church provides women with the hope and motivation that they need to survive in such a context.

The fathers also lose out in all of this, because by excluding themselves from the family sphere (while simultaneously presenting themselves as "head of the family" in regards to the outside observers), it is very difficult for them to maintain healthy relationships with their wives and children. Having delegated the daily responsibilities of raising their children to their spouses, they are rarely at home and know little about what goes on there. Hence it is difficult for them to take on the role of "He who Knows All and therefore Decides and Controls." So... when a problem arises, and to "regain a little order" as soon as possible and preserve his social image of the good "patriarch," the father will pound his fist on the table and impose his "peace" by means of threats and/or guilt. The French call this method of conflict resolution "faire la Paix Romaine" ("Pax Romana", see insert below). But the intimidating show of force only introduces an additional malaise in familial relationships and increases the relational difficulties already present.

---

Definition of **PAX ROMANA** (Latin for "Roman Peace"): **"1.** The comparative peace brought about by Roman rule over the Mediterranean world (27 B.C.-A.D. 180) **2.** Any such relatively peaceful political condition resulting from the dominance of a large power."

Cf. Webster's New World Dictionary, Fourth Edition, Wiley Publishing, Inc

---

Regarding children, it is important to highlight the extent of suffering that *patriarchal matriarchy* causes:

Assuming that the mother is an autonomous adult (in the best-case scenario), she will try to raise her children towards autonomy. But if her husband lacks personal autonomy – demanding to be *served* in the daily tasks of life – he will not encourage his children in this direction (at least, not the ones he considers "superior," like him). Thus, he will discredit his wife when she tries to educate the children towards autonomy, requesting that they "carry their weight" (by participating in the daily chores, for example). If the father discredits her here, she will find herself having to *serve/assist* both her husband *and* her children (especially those "covered" by the father). The children will grow up to expect someone to serve them. Thus the cycle perpetuates itself from generation to generation.

Conversely, if the mother is a frustrated, "castrated," non-autonomous woman (because she was deprived of her right to achieve her personal, social and professional ambitions), she will face great difficulty in raising her children in a healthy manner. Persecuted by the various "authorities" who reigned over her and imposed themselves on her—using all the unhealthy games mentioned above—she lives in fear and bitterness. Having the "obligation" to handle the household, she must raise her children in a world that frightens her. So she over-protects her children and sets out to manage, decide and control everything. In the father's absence (which is most of the time), she acts alone, projecting onto her children all her obsessions and anxieties. If she doesn't have the strength and personality to take on such a demanding role, she will call on her eldest to assist her in the task.

The husband, who purposely remains "exterior" to of all this—occupying an "external" position (from where criticism is easy)—reigns "from above." From this "superior position," he can gain his children's respect, without having to engage in (or commit himself to) any of the difficult educative tasks. This leaves the mother with all the unpleasant tasks of parenting, along with all the children's eventual resentments (encouraged and fostered by the father's lack of support).

And as described earlier, in this patriarchal context where it is most important to uphold the *Chef's* image (where everyone must appear strong and happy in order to maintain the pretension that the "head of the family" is infallible), everyone avoids expressing their difficulties. Not expressed openly, people's needs are expressed indirectly, covertly (by manipulating, building strategies, conspiring, etc.). Much happens secretly, "under the table," behind closed doors. Hidden agendas rule the scene.

One strives to keep the "image" (seen from the outside) intact, while on the inside the atmosphere is full of unspoken turmoil. The children grow up in the obscurity of hidden messages, fearful of reprisals that may be inflicted upon them from having misunderstood what was truly expected of them. Extensive personal work is required to escape such relational disorder.

And, in the final run, the blame for the children's consequential mental or behavioral disorder will be put on the mothers. And interestingly enough, the first to blame mothers are psychologists and religious clergymen...

\*\*\*\*\*\*\*\*\*\*\*\*\*\*\*

In France, there are many books written about women's tears and why this gender cries so much and so often. Statistics are put forth, noting that women suffer more from depression than men. There seems to be much research done to understand this phenomenon. All kinds or neurological, hormonal, genetic (etc.) explanations have been presented as to why women cry, why they are so emotional. Some say that it is just "nature": that the female brain is just made that way....

Is it so difficult to comprehend why women cry more often than men? It is not perfectly natural to cry when one is hurt and hurt when one is treated unfairly? No, there is no mystery there. The truth is so simple, yet so few seem to admit it. The capacity humans have to deny what they do not want to see, ignore what they find inconvenient or uncomfortable, and/or repute what doesn't fit in their scheme of things, is most disconcerting...

The female condition is very relevant to the subject of this book. It is actually at the heart of the problem. Yes, the way people treat each other in a society is directly associated to the way women are treated at home, in that same society.

It is worth noting that the economically prosperous societies are those where men and women share mutual respect and consideration. Glaring statistics in this area show that in societies where women are professionally engaged (not only at the service level but also in management), professional opportunities are better distributed within the population, and power is shared more equitably. Personal and creative initiatives seem to be greeted with greater enthusiasm. New ideas are more easily embraced and better accommodations are made for the newcomers. The presence of women in organizations seems to moderate the male desire for *exclusivity*. The right to being different and tolerance for those "not like everyone else" is more prevalent. It is a simple fact that societies that foster cooperation in parenthood do better (economically) than the societies that legitimize the control of one parent over the other (and one child over the others).

In patriarchal cultures, *exclusivity* reigns. The right to speak and the power to act belong only those authorized, who monopolize all initiatives and subsequently block economic development.

# CONCLUSION

It is important to note that the way men treat women in a society (whether imposing themselves on them or cooperating with them) has direct consequences on the way people treat each other in that society. And the way parents treat each other has a direct effect on how their children go on to treat their peers.

> The feminist movement in the 1970s had the slogan "the personal is political." Those women clearly understood this particular issue and knew that their struggle largely surpassed their own gender situation. Their call for change was to make the world a better place, *for everyone.*

Rejection or acceptance of differences begins in the home, in the relationship between parents (how fathers and mothers manage their differences), between parents and their children, and between the siblings themselves. Given that many children grow in families where (1) the father imposes his will upon all the other members of the family (2) the mother acts as sergeant when the general is out (3) the parents (more or less anguished and/or frustrated) try to force the cultural traditions onto the children (via negative strokes, humiliations and/or threats) all while protecting themselves of any mutual or reciprocal questioning (to preserve their "infallibility")... it is not surprising that many people in this world kill to dominate (without the least questioning of their own destructive power).

Yes, through authoritarian behaviors, we make our children believe huge lies: that some people know it all, are infallible, cannot be questioned, and that it is OK for them to bully others to get what they want. In the name of some kind of religious or political "authority," they are authorized to do as they please (using strategies of intimidation) and are entitled to our blind trust, loyalty and obedience.

Unfortunately, the Law-of-the-strongest of the patriarchal paradigm *is not* reserved to our belle France. And no French person that I know strives for it. Many of my French patriots (probably most) strive for the contrary, hoping for greater justice in our country, and in the world. I am deeply convinced that we are not consciously perpetuating this dysfunctional system and are not hurting one another on purpose. I am also convinced that everyone loses from this system (some obviously lose more than others) and that even the *chefs,* though privileged by the system, suffer deeply from it, because of the harm that it does to their personal relationships.

I know many French people who work—sweat and tears— to bring relief to the "underdogs" of the system. I deeply admire their persistence in the task and it pains me to see them wear themselves out in the undertaking. I hope that this analysis of the French malaise offers them an enlightening perspective on the subject and a better understanding of the grounds on which they operate. Hopefully, this book will give them greater strength in their struggle for justice.

Understanding the history of this enormous struggle— which seems to have accompanied humanity since its origins—can offer us a better understanding of the violence that still occurs within our own country. May this awareness help us discover new pathways **to liberty and justice for all**.

Cultural mindsets and behaviors have been modeled by linguistic constructions that drive our thoughts. However, since our languages change over time, the concepts and ideas they convey also change.

This applies to concept of LAW, for example, that has varied over time. Its evolution can be traced through writings left to us by many thinkers over thousands of years. Among these texts, the Bible is the most famous. It has modeled the entire Judeo-Christian culture, which is ours today. My linguistic analysis of the Bible leads me to believe that the concept of LAW, constantly evolving over centuries and civilizations, has historically been— and still is today—at the heart of our cultural conflicts.

# I. THE CONCEPT OF LAW IN THE BIBLE

## A. THE LAW AS "COVENANT" (THE GIVEN WORD)

The term for law in Hebrew is "Torah", name given by the Jews to the Mosaic Law (referring to Moses). Torah is the title of the Jewish sacred book that lays out behavioral rules in Jewish society. The Jewish people, concerned about their survival as an entity in the Diaspora (they were dispersed in various regions of the Middle East), treasured their Covenant with their God and were very concerned about transmitting it to their children and grandchildren.

For Jews, the Law is a covenant (an alliance) that God (Yahweh) forged with his people. He gave them his word (His Promise) and a *promise of heritage* (through Abraham). Yahweh

("The Un-named"), is He who establishes *authority*. His Law is a written law. "The Ark of the Covenant" symbolizes the *God Given Word* to the chosen people and embodies this Written Law. "Doctors of Law" would take on the vocation of *transmitting (transcribing, translating, interpreting, etc.)* the sacred texts of the "Given Word" and the Promise of Alliance/Covenant.

---

The word CONVENANT (*"Berit"* in Hebrew, meaning *"in between"*)

"…is one of the most frequently used terms in the Old Testament (289 times), so often that many authors have thought it to be the key concept that unifies the whole Bible; giving its name, by the way, to the two parts of the Christian Bible. Without a doubt, this is true; but only if one understands the difficulties of its translation. Most French translators translate it to *alliance* (covenant)…

Whatever it may be, *berit* is always based on a bond between two partners, but their involvement is not the same. … With Abraham (Gen. 15:17–18), only God is involved, and unconditionally, in support of Noah and his descendants. On the contrary, the covenant with Moses in the Sinaï is a reciprocal one, conditioned to its fidelity to Israel (Ex. 24:1–11)…"

Cf. *La Bible et sa culture*, ed. Desclée de Brouwer, 2000

---

## B. THE LAW AS "DIATHEKE" (THE SHARED WORD)

With early Christianity, certain texts from the Torah (the Jewish sacred Book) were selected to constitute the first part of the Christian Bible. These texts, today known as the "Old Testament", were then enriched by new texts written in Greek (today known as the "New Testament"). Greek was the language common to the eastern Mediterranean Basin, at the time, and these Christian texts, written in Greek, were called "Diatheke."

The Greeks, who had already reflected on the virtues of personal expression (thanks to Socrates and his successors) and had implemented practical applications (democratic practices), had a slightly different concept of Law and Alliance. So the Greek speaking Christians integrated the concept of God's Given Word/Covenant/"Promise of Alliance" in their own way:

In Greek, "diatheke" means "transmission/diffusion/sharing of the word" (*dia* = share, *theke* = word*).* The Greek Christians chose this term to designate the transmission of their religious heritage (God's Given Covenant/Alliance) because "diatheke" represented the legal act through which the Greeks passed on their material heritage from one generation to another.

It is very interesting to note that in ancient Greece, the transmission of the inheritance only occurred once the heir had confirmed his affiliation to the deceased. The son could take possession of his inheritance only upon producing an act of acknowledgement, recognizing his alliance with his deceased father. This gesture of acknowledgement, carried out by the receiving beneficiary, created a bilateral dimension to the act of transmission. The legal interaction thus resembles a kind of mutually recognized covenant.

The God of Hebraic LAW (*the Given Word*) was thus transformed into a God of the Shared Word (*Diatheke*), transmitted only to those who have actively affirmed their affiliation by showing a sign of recognition and acceptance. The narratives from the *Diatheke* ("New Testament") describe a man named Jesus who baptized and cared for those who requested it of him. His services went to all those who recognized him as "the son of God" (even beyond the Jewish community). The Gospels (Biblical texts written around Jesus' life) seem to emphasize the importance of the personal and voluntary step made by the beneficiary in this "new Covenant with God" (a God who presents Himself as a God of Love and Mutual Recognition). Thus a connection between faith, love, mutual recognition and personal commitment was forged.

However, this new Biblical concept of bilateral commitment

(alliance by voluntary and mutual consent) was quickly shrouded by an erroneous Latin translation of the Greek texts. It would remain shrouded for a very long time, nearly 1500 years! Not until the 16th century (with a rediscovery of the Bible in its original languages) would it reappear in the Christian faith.

## C. THE LAW AS "TESTAMENT" (THE IMPOSED WORD)

These same texts (Torah + Diatheke)—which, roughly speaking, constitute the Old and the New Testament—were brought together to constitute the "Bible" (which means "The Book," in Latin). And as Latin became the language common to the Mediterranean Basin (with the spreading of the Roman Empire), the Bible was translated into Latin. But the Romans had yet another concept of Law and Alliance, and this difference transpired in the Latin translations of the Bible:

The Latin theologians translated the Greek word *Diatheke* by the word *Testament*, because that was their word for the legal act of transmitting an inheritance. However, unlike the Greeks, the Romans dealt with the transmission of inheritance in a vertical and unilateral manner. It was the donor who acknowledged his heir (and not the heir that acknowledged his affiliation with the donor). Property was passed on through an act of designation by the donor to the recipient. The testament was thus a unilateral commitment, made by the deceased (the transmitter), to the person of his choosing (the recipient). This handing over of property to the designated recipient was based on a unilateral decision-making process. The chosen heir was designated, whether he liked it or not.

Hence, in Latin culture, one does not choose one's inheritance (what is being transmitted to him/her), nor can he/she avoid it. It is imposed. One cannot refuse that which is given to him/her. Acceptance is mandatory. One does not say "no." This concept of imposed law/covenant/alliance (that I will henceforth designate as "unilateral law") generates relational violence since it discounts the opinion of the receiver in favor of that of the transmitter. The two parties are not considered on an equal basis, legitimizing relationships of domination/submission. This system is quite discriminating and dangerously unfair, particularly when entire categories of people are designated as "The Transmitters," while other categories are attributed the role of "Recipients."

The progression thus went from the Jewish "Given Word" to the Christian "Shared Word" to the Catholic "Imposed Word."

It is not surprising that the Romans found it difficult to translate the idea of *Diatheke*, because they were not equipped to understand the concept of mutual consent. Roman society, highly centralized and organized from top to bottom (in a pyramidal hierarchal structure), could only conceive of LAW coming from above. There were those who dictated the orders and others who were to carry them out. It was out of the question to ask "subordinates" for their opinion!

The etymology of the verb *OBEIR* (French for "to obey") clearly reveals the unilateral approach to communication in the Latin culture:

---

"The French word *Obeir* (to obey) comes from the Latin word *audire* (to listen). The verb *audire* (to listen) becomes *ouïr* in French (to hear).

The Latin verb *oboedire*, composed of *audire* and the prefix *ob-* (in face of) means 'to listen to someone's opinion,' 'to be submitted to him/her.' In French, it became *obéir*."

Quoted from *Etymologies du français*, by René Garrus

---

For more than one thousand years (until the onset of the

Renaissance) France, under the aegis of the Roman Catholic Church, functioned exclusively under this concept of the LAW: dictated from "on high," unilaterally, by certain beings who claim to have authority over others, and who demand submission and obedience. These many years of Roman Catholic reign over Europe constitute the period that historians call "The Dark Ages".

# II. AN INTELLECTUAL REVOLUTION

## A. THE RENAISSANCE

The start of the 15<sup>th</sup> century brought on an intellectual, political and religious revolution that would shake up the entire European continent. Burning questions about power, the abuse of power and the power of knowledge would feed passionate debates in Europe for several centuries:

- **Who** embodies authority: *the Church or Science?*
- **Who** constitutes the Church: *the people or the clergy?*
- **Who** decides who makes Law: *God, men or men of God?*
- **What** does Divine Law call for: *obligatory service or service of free will?*

These important philosophical, political and religious issues—that ultimately divided Europe in two—are rooted in a combination of historical circumstances that questioned the dogmas of the Roman Catholic Church (supreme authority of the times). Listed below are a few that had a profound historical impact:

1. The invention of the printing press (1434), which provided greater diffusion of knowledge to "common mortals." Thanks to this invention, the Book of Divine Law (the Bible, considered the "Word of God") became accessible to a greater number of people. But this popularization of the Bible triggered violent reactions (including torture and homicide) from the Roman clergy, who held exclusivity over "God's Sacred Word" and had no intention of sharing its exclusive right to reading and interpreting the Bible.

2. <u>The fall of Constantinople (1453)</u>, which led to the Diaspora of great linguistic scholars, fleeing to various European capitals. These scholars brought with them their knowledge of "ancient" languages, giving Europe the opportunity to rediscover the original languages of the Biblical texts (Greek, Hebrew and Aramaic). This led to new interpretations of the Bible. Reread in its original languages and then retranslated into the various "vernacular" languages (the commonly spoken languages of the times), the freshly translated Bible revealed new ideas. The long forgotten **bilateral** dimension of Covenant—an idea that remained in the "oubliettes" (the forgotten place) during fifteen centuries of Latin domination—was reintroduced into Christianity. This rediscovery gave birth to new theological concepts and new ecclesiastical practices, questioning the traditional church structure. Thus, as a consequence of this newly rediscovered *bilateral* notion, many Christians distanced themselves from the Roman Catholic Church and new religious movements ("churches") sprouted throughout Europe.

3. <u>The discovery of other lands in the world</u> which opened Europe to new intellectual (cultural, philosophical and religious) perspectives, including:
   - Antilles by Columbus (1492)
   - North American Continent by Cabot (1497)
   - South American Continent by Cabrol (1500)
   - Trip around the African Continent by Gama (1497–1498)
   - Trip around the world by Magellan and del Cano (1519–1522)

4. <u>A popular movement of indignation against the Pope (1517)</u> which would forever split the Christian community. This movement of "protest" (that gave birth to the "Protestant" movement) was set off by a Catholic monk named Martin Luther who revolted against the abuses of his church. At the

time, the Roman Catholic Church was threatening its followers with suffering in the Afterlife if they did not observe its orders of "good conduct." This they had done for over a thousand years. But now they were setting out to offer *relief* from that Afterlife suffering in exchange for money. Hence, those who paid were "relieved" of some of the punishments in their afterlife. This relief (called "indulgences") was the Vatican's way of getting the money it needed to pay for the construction of Saint Peter's Basilica in Rome. Martin Luther's vivid expression of indignation against these methods was widely supported by many Christians all across Europe and came to seriously question Rome's Authority. Many politicians also seized the opportunity to settle their accounts with the Roman Catholic clergy.

5. Copernicus' heliocentric theory, printed in 1543, which would set off a scientific revolution. The Copernican theory affirmed that the earth revolves around the sun (instead of the contrary, as was then believed). Despite all scientific evidence confirming this theory, Copernicus's theory would be virulently disputed by the Catholic Church as being "opposed to the Scriptures." (The Church wished to maintain Man as the center of the universe...)

Historians have designated this entire period of intellectual upheaval as *The Renaissance*. Indeed, by shaking up the Roman Catholic Church's monolithic frame of reference, these events opened Europe to new fields of exploration, providing great opportunities for intellectual "rebirth" ("Renaissance" in French literally means "rebirth"). Europe experienced an explosion of creativity in all of the arts: music, architecture, painting, etc. As Europe was making these many discoveries, it entered a new age of intellectual enlightenment, leaving behind a millennium of Dark Ages. The European Continent was shedding its old skin.

Changes in the balance of power, however, rarely occur without violent upheavals. Vital issues – raised tenaciously by the Humanists (philosophers) and the Reformers (theologians) – shook all of Europe. In France, those who protested against ecclesiastic authority would pay dearly for their questioning and for their disagreement. Religious wars (and the ensuing Inquisition) would bring death, exile or abjuration to all those who protested against the imposed, unilateral concept of Latin law.

## B. The Reformation

- Who were the *Protestants*?

The Protestants were Western European Christians who *protested* against the clergy's abuse of power in the Roman Catholic Church. They asserted their right, as laymen (non-clergymen), to have direct access to God and to God's Word (the Bible). Up until then, Roman Catholic clergymen had kept the Bible to themselves, forbidding access to "the Word of God" to any "non ordained" person. The Protestants, on the other hand, believed that the "Word of God" was intended for *all* baptized Christians, and not just an elite few. So they translated the Bible into everyday language, making it understandable by all, and they gathered in spontaneous, informal meetings to read it together (in hiding, of course, to avoid reprisals from the Roman clergy). They taught their children to read to give them direct access to "God's Word".

Thus, by reading the Bible in versions that had been directly translated from the original languages, these people rediscovered the bilateral dimension of "diatheke" (the concept of *bilateral* engagement in the Sacred Covenant.) This rediscovery had an enormous impact on their understanding of the Scriptures and seriously amplified their detachment from the Roman Catholic Church. It pushed them to the point of formulating a new

"Reformed" theology. According to their new reading of the Biblical texts (that presented the Sacred Alliance as being valid *only if sealed by an act of acknowledgement on the part of the receiver),* these people believed that one is not *born* a Christian, but *becomes* a Christian, through active, voluntary, personal choice.

This new understanding of the Scriptures (with its emphasis on *voluntary adhesion)* introduced a whole new concept in religion: free will. Man was henceforth granted the freedom to say "yes" or "no" to his God. This revolutionary theological concept would have significant repercussions on future societies; because with the freedom to choose man takes hold of his personal destiny. With the right to say "yes" or "no" and to make his own choices, he becomes responsible for his own life.

Another major breakthrough was that no one could henceforth force someone else into being a Christian. The alliance to God could only occur with the person's explicit agreement. In other words, free consent was now required for binding a commitment. The covenant no longer occurs without mutual and reciprocal acknowledgement between the two parties. The Protestants refusal to baptize young children (in favor of adult baptism) is an example of their attachment to *Free Will* and *mutual consent.*

By reading the new Biblical translations (that were more faithful to the Greek writings), these same "protestors" affirmed that God is in fact the God of all, for all those who recognize Him as such. According to them, making a personal and voluntary step (a step that only the individual himself could make, and that no one else could make for him) was enough to seal his Alliance with God. They also proclaimed that all Christians stand equal before God and that they are all brothers of One and the Same Father. Thus, they refuted the church's hierarchy, affirming that there was no other Father/Author/Creator other than God-the-Father, and no *Lord* other than the Lord God. Priests were therefore no longer recognized as "fathers" and the bishops were no longer called "My Lord." No one could henceforth claim to be the "author" of anyone else's life. The Protestants professed "universal *sacerdose*" for all those who were baptized (*sacerdose*[8] means "priesthood" in Latin).

No longer could anyone claim "authority" (superiority) over his fellow man within the community of believers. This theological difference still stands as a barrier between Catholics and Protestants today, and continues to express itself vividly in the ecumenical debates.

---

This point in history marks the disappearance of the distinction between "you" and "thou" in the English language. "You" (corresponding to the French formal "*vous*") would henceforth be used to address everyone, thus giving each person full and equal consideration/respect. And the informal "Thou" would be reserved exclusively to God.

The Quaker movement—born out of these important religious, political and social issues in the middle of the 17th century in England—continues today to practice this ideal of **brotherhood/ equality before God.** Everyone was given an equal voice, and there were no longer any titles given to anyone: no more religious hierarchy (no clergy) nor social hierarchy.

"*If God is directly accessible to all persons, regardless of age, gender, race, nationality, economic, social or educational position - if every person is held equal in God's love and has equal potential to be a channel for the revelation of God's Truth - then all persons are to be equally valued. There is that Seed, that Light - there is "that of God" in every person. For Friends this insight has meant, from the beginning, equality of the sexes and of races.*

Excerpt from a Quaker website "An Introduction to Quakers"
http://emes.quaker.eu.org

---

8     Cf. *The Pocket Oxford Latin Dictionary*, Oxford University Press, 1994

- France and the Protestants

France was deeply affected by this theological and philosophical revolution spreading throughout all of Northern Europe. A large number of citizens were attracted to this intellectual movement towards equality. A Frenchman from Picardy, known as John Calvin, was one of the great "institutors" of this movement, known as the Reformation (because it called for a *reformation* of the Church). John Calvin, along with his Scottish counterpart John Knox, proposed a new institutional structure for the church that was more adapted to the principle of "all equal before God." His proposed structure evenly divided the decision-making power among all the members of the church community. He completely reversed the Latin pyramidal structure, rendering all decision-making power to the base. He advocated that *all decisions* concerning the community of followers were to be made by *all of the community members.* Each local community then designated a representative who would serve as their "spokesman" for the "synods" (which were regional gatherings of all the representatives from the various local communities).

It is precisely on this democratic institutional model that the Democratic Republic of the United States was to be conceived 200 years later on the "new continent." And this "synodal-presbyterian" system continues to function this way in the Reformed Church of France and in the Scottish Presbyterian Church today.

During the Reformation (the 16<sup>th</sup> and 17<sup>th</sup> centuries), some European countries completely turned toward Protestantism. However France, far too deeply engaged in the Latin hierarchical system, could not allow for such questioning of its power structures. France thus chose to maintain its hierarchical system of *Vertical law* with its pyramidal structure and pushed many

French Protestants beyond its boundaries (and also into the Seine River: it is said that the Seine River actually turned red from all the blood that was shed). By ridding itself of the Protestants, France also rid itself of this "heresy" of Bilateral Law; an ideal that would continue to develop elsewhere—mostly in England—and that would eventually lead to the future proclamations for Human Rights (see the annex for a the list of documents that lead up to the great Declaration of the Human Rights).

- Protestants and the "New World"

The persecuted Protestants, in an attempt to escape the tyranny of the Counter-Reformation of Roman Catholic Europe, fled to the new American continent, recently discovered by European explorers. They crossed the Atlantic, hoping to settle there in peace. Upon arrival, they organized themselves politically to set up a system of public order that was consistent with their principle of "all equal before God."

---

The concepts of' universal suffrage' and 'all equal' did not, at the time, include either women or Black people (who were not regarded as full-fledged citizens). As for the indigenous people of the new continent (the Native Americans), they were barely considered members of the larger human family. They were assigned a separate status, socially, politically and geographically.

It wasn't until much later that the Black male population and then the entire female population gained the right to vote: 1870 for Black men (via the 15th Amendment of the Constitution) and 1920 for women (via the 19th Amendment). And to obtain this right to vote, both used the same arguments, underlining the concept of equality. The Southern states (a region of the US largely of French and Catholic influence), however, posed great resistance to actually exercising that right.

One hundred years later, Martin Luther King, Jr., a Protestant pastor in the Southern United States would reaffirm "all equal before God" to fight the persisting racism and associated discrimination.

---

But...how can public order be maintained if no one can claim "authority" over his fellow man? The answer was found in the democratic institution constituted by the Reformers. The religious claim of "equal access to the Word" was translated onto the political level by universal suffrage (that wasn't truly universal, as the inset above specifies). This system granted each white man an **equal voice** in any decisions that regarded the entire group. No one—*regardless of his personal, familial, professional or financial resources*—could claim to have a predominant voice. Hence, decision making became the fruit of the "shared word," with equal say. Decisions would be made by way of <u>secret</u> ballot, safe from eventual retaliation. From this voting process—founded on the principle of equal voice for all white males—laws were legislated, rules were set, and social order was established.

# III. POLITICAL REVOLUTIONS

## A. THE AMERICAN REVOLUTION

In order to implement a new form of government more consistent with the principles of free will, free choice and a voice for all, the inhabitants of the New World declared their independence from the English Crown (to which they had were still "subjects"). They then set up their own system of government.

To avoid reproducing a *totalitarian* and *dictatorial* State, where all power is granted to one individual (a system they had known elsewhere and had fled), the revolutionaries of the new continent chose to separate the State powers into three distinct and independent bodies: 1) the Legislative Power, 2) the Executive Power and 3) the Judicial Power. Each body is separate but dependent on the other two. This separation of Powers would be the cornerstone of the political edifice, guaranteeing long-term stability.

It was also agreed that the Legislative power could not promulgate a law without express consent of all the citizens. So a voting system (by universal suffrage) was set that guaranteed voter approval to any new proposed law. This was the visible affirmation that no one, any longer, could "make Law" over any other individual. The Law could never be anything other than the product of group discussion, *shared speech (with equal voices)* between all those concerned.

The founding fathers of the American Constitution formulated this new, completely revolutionary system of government, in collaboration with some of the great French philosophers, with whom they were in close contact. Thus was born, in 1776, the "Democratic Republic of the United States".

## B. THE FRENCH REVOLUTION

During the period of Enlightenment, the great French Humanists (Voltaire 1694–1778, Montesquieu 1689–1755, Diderot 1713–1784, Rousseau 1712–1778, etc.) introduced concepts of *Human Rights* into France that were already largely present in England. These French intellectuals were deeply influenced by the writings of earlier English thinkers (Roger Bacon 1214–1294, Francis Bacon 1561–1626, Hobbes 1588–1679, Locke 1632–1704, etc.).

There was constant exchange between France and England regarding issues of individual rights. The humanistic spirit crossed the borders regularly (in both directions). Most of the philosophers mentioned above had crossed the Channel to spend time in the neighboring country. These *"voyages"* created opportunities for mutual influence. The Magna Carta, the first English document that prefigures all other Human Rights documents, was actually first drafted *in France* (where the English "subjects" found refuge to express their demands to their king).

In the scientific domain, exchanges were also constant between the two countries. Encounters occurred mostly by chance. But they also occurred thanks to the efforts of certain individuals, who were convinced of the importance of cooperation in this domain.

---

The monk Marin Mersenne (1588–1648), a French philosopher who was highly influenced by the contributions of Galileo and convinced of the necessity for collective scientific work, undertook to promote exchanges between all scholars of his time (Descartes, Pascal, Fermat, Beckmann and Torricelli). He visited them and maintained prolific correspondence with them. His work is an example of international scientific cooperation.

---

The documents enforced in England concerning individual freedoms and their institutional guarantees—based on citizen protection and the rights of the people (common law) vis-à-vis the authority of the Crown—exerted a profound influence on French revolutionary thinkers. The great French intellectuals walked "hand-in-hand"—philosophically and politically—with their English counterparts from across both the Channel and the Atlantic. France would thus engage in its own experience of political revolution, only a few years after the American Revolution: in 1789, the French people rebelled against their king (the privileged heir to *Vertical Law* and *"Chef"* by "divine right").

It is interesting to note that the French Revolution's motto, *"Liberté, Egalité, Fraternité"* (which literally means "liberty, equality, brotherhood"), comes from three ideas inspired by the Reformation, which claimed freedom (of speech), equality (of speech) and brotherhood (all *brothers* under One Father).

Moreover, the claim of "all equal" is a partial duplication (a secular version) of the Protestant claim of "all equal before God" (*all equally* respected and *all equally* considered). However, eliminating the words "before God" in the secular version seriously distorts the meaning, suggesting equality in *ability*, which is totally unrealistic. The original idea was to aim for equal *opportunity* (not equal *capacity!*), so that everyone could develop his or her own *abilities* (that *differ* from one person to another).

For their emancipation, the French people referred to the model of government that was established across the Atlantic (to which they had actively contributed). They then reiterated the essence of the Declaration of Independence of the United States of America in their "Declaration of the Rights of Man and of the Citizen" that they proclaimed on 26 August 1789. Unfortunately, this 1789 Declaration would have no normative value at the time of its proclamation; it would take 150 years before holding any constitutional value (through the Preamble of the Constitution of 27 October 1946).

However, contrary to the basic principle on which the American Constitution was founded (*"power to the people, by the people and for the people"*), the legislators of the French Constitution chose a monarchical framework for their new government: On 9 July 1789, the National Constituent Assembly put an end to absolutism in favor of a *Constitutional Monarchy*. Once again, in order to protect the authority of the "enlightened" elite, France chose the traditional framework of *vertical law*.

Subsequently, the political power granted to the people amounted to basically nothing. And though the Constitution of the Convention (1793–1795) foresaw the application of "universal suffrage" in legislative elections and established the use of referendums, this Constitution never was applied.

The bloody period of the Terror that followed the French Revolution brought about several years of chaos and power relationships. This chaos would discredit the new government and destroy any remaining hope of creating a real political democracy. The principles of liberty and freedom of speech (equal right to speak up and to be heard), sown by the Revolution of 1789, would be swept away from the French landscape in just a few years:

On 18 and 19 Brumaire (9 and 10 November) 1799, an army general, Napoleon Bonaparte (aided by the army) staged a "coup d'état" and installed a provisional government. Then in 1804, he crowned himself the Emperor of France (a very Latin method) and had the Pope Pie VII consecrate him Emperor of France in the grand Cathedral of Notre Dame in Paris (thus, imitating Charlemagne, who sealed his alliance with the Church of Rome by having himself crowned Emperor of the West by the Pope, 25 December 800).

Within a short time, this soldier from Corsica (of Latin culture, once again!) destroyed the few remaining democratic concepts left in France and reintroduced the dimension of "divine right." This military general set up State institutions that resembled military structures (based on vertical relationships from superiors to inferiors). The entire political organization was one highly centralized power unit in the form of a pyramidal structure of hierarchies, with Napoleon himself placed alone at the top.

The family unit (as well as religious, economic and social institutions) was ordered by law to comply with this same logic of hierarchy (dominant/submissive relationship model). The 1804 Napoleonic Code of 1804 placed a married woman under the authority of her husband. She would be considered "incapable and a minor for life":

> "Unlike the adult unmarried woman, who is considered to be competent, it is impossible for a wife to take legal action or to exercise any right without her husband's consent. The principle of citizenship, so concerned with equality, did not seem to affect the condition of married women: "people deprived of rights are: minors, married women, criminals and the mentally disabled" (Art. 1124).
>
> Marital guardianship, which implies that a married woman can neither work nor hold a bank account without her husband's consent, was the rule. Similarly, the wife could not conceal her private correspondence from her husband, nor act freely in her relationships or movement. And these are only a few examples."[9]

---

[9]    Cf. *Livre de Notre Mariage*, ed. Evénements et Tendances, Paris 2005. This little booklet, that is today handed out by some City Governments to young couples getting married, exposes (as does this passage) some past civil codes on marriages in France.

Then, under the regime of the Consulate and the First Empire (1799–1815), the question of "universal suffrage" was completely dropped. However, the Consular Constitution of 22 Frimaire in year VIII allowed recourse to the plebiscite (referendum), which Napoleon Bonaparte frequently used to change the Constitution and ultimately install the imperial regime.

**************

The next constitutional monarchy (1815–1848) was still not a government based on "universal suffrage." It was a *censitaire* system (a regime based on "censitaire suffrage.") "Censitaire suffrage" means that the right to vote is based on wealth. Thus, the only citizens (i.e. males) who could vote were those wealthy enough to do so. And they voted to elect their government representatives, who, in turn imposed their laws. The King would remain at the top of the country, representing the *Supreme Authority* (a concept that was no longer questioned).

**************

With the Constitution of the Second Republic (1848–1852), "universal suffrage" was finally adopted (it was called "universal," but it excluded the women, the military, the clergy and the Algerians)[10], allowing for the election of the President of the Republic. However, the Second Republic did not last long. Vertical logic rapidly took over, and within four years, the new President of the Republic proclaimed himself Emperor:

---

[10]    Cf. http://fr.wikipedia.org/wiki/Suffrage_universel

> "As President of the French Republic and in opposition to the conservative Assembly, Louis-Napoleon organized a Coup d'Etat on 2 December 1851 that allowed him to impose a new constitution and soon to impose a French Empire. The first half of this "Second Empire" is called the Authoritarian Empire. ...
>
> The Constitution of 14 January 1852 instituted by Napoleon III was largely inspired by the one of the year VIII. Despite the re-establishment of universal male suffrage, executive powers remained concentrated in the hands of the Head of State. He could name members of the State Council (who were responsible for preparing laws) and of the Senate (a body permanently established as a constitutional part of the Empire). The legislative body was once again elected, by universal male suffrage; however, it had no right to take any initiative; all laws were to be proposed by the executive power."
>
> Cf. http://frwikipedia.org/wiki/Suffrageuniversel, citation 7 nov 2007

Consequently, France fell back into a dictatorial, quasi-totalitarian regime... for nearly 20 years (1852–1870).

**************

As for the Third Republic (1875–1940), it would apply "universal suffrage" (for males) but only to give the French males very limited freedom of choice, and only in the political realm. They could now elect the members of the National Assembly and of the Senate[11], but saw very minimal change in their freedom to take personal initiatives in their everyday lives. The liberty to express oneself and take personal initiatives in other areas of society was exclusively reserved to a privileged few: those designated as "trustworthy" (based on the very restricted criteria of "contributive value"). These people would continue to monopolize the right to think and to take initiative, dictating their

---

11

will upon others, forcing them into submission (and abuse). Thus, the large majority of French people remained "subjects" of the political "authorities", with very little leeway to act of their own behalf.

It was precisely this rigid and suffocating social context (which proved quite disappointing after the high hopes of freedom triggered by the Revolution 100 years earlier) that French intellectuals offered the *Statue of Liberty* to their "revolutionary brothers" across the Atlantic. It was their way of expressing their disappointment and renewing their commitment to freedom.

The magnificent *Liberty Enlightening the World*, more commonly known as the Statue of Liberty, was dedicated in 1886 and placed in New York, in the largest port of entry in the United States. Liberty was here portrayed by a woman, standing upright and holding a tablet in her left hand (representing Knowledge) and a lighted torch in her right hand (representing Enlightenment).

"The Statue of Liberty was sculpted by French sculptor Frederic-Auguste Bartholdi, and its internal structure was engineered by Gustave Eiffel. The idea of presenting a gift as a gesture of Franco-American friendship to mark the one-hundredth anniversary of the country's independence is attributed to the politician and historian Édouard Lefebvre de Laboulaye, author of *Paris in America* and *Contes Bleus*. Bartholdi confided to his friend Lefebvre de Laboulaye:

*'I shall fight for liberty; I shall call for freedom of the people. I will work for the glory of that Republic there, until the day I find it here, once again.'*"

Cf. http://fr.wikipedia.org/wiki/Statue_de_Liberte

Concerned about being a too rigid in the area of cultural activities, France adopted new legislation in 1901 that allowed its citizens to organize themselves locally into "associations."

Through these local organizations (called *les associations à loi 1901*/Associations under the 1901 Law), people gained room for expression and freedom of movement at the local level. Unfortunately, within their sphere of action, most of these associations would adopt the dictatorial mode of functioning practiced in all the other French social structures. They followed the hierarchal model, reserving the power of reflection and decision making to one single individual (the President, often self-designated), or to a small committee of individuals (the body officers, often self-designated). Still today, an association that applies true elections of its representatives and grants a genuine stake in reflection, decision making and freedom of initiative to all of its members remains rare.

Until the Second World War, the majority of the French population—the entire female population—continued to be reduced to silence and deprived of participation in the realm of politics. Yes, only during the latter part of the Third Republic—and because of the devastation caused by the War—would the French women finally be recognized as adult members of the nation. Freed of the restrictions and prohibitions imposed upon them during "normal times," the French women took great initiatives during World War II and showed undeniable effectiveness in social affairs. Thus, in 1944, they were acknowledged as full-fledged citizens and included in the "universal suffrage" that voted for the Constitution of the Fourth Republic (1946–1958).

The fact that the French women were among the last of the Western world to be politically emancipated (i.e. allowed to *speak up* in political affairs) should raise serious questions for us. Here, below, are a few historical facts that expose our cultural misogyny (sexism, discrimination against women):

The first 10 regions of the world to lift the ban against women's participation in elections were all English speaking regions (the only exception was the Republic of Corsica, which oddly enough, was the very first to officially give the women the right to vote – in 1755. France, however, abolished this right (that was only granted to non-married Corsican women) as soon as it annexed the island in 1769.

- State of New Jersey (USA): in 1776
- Pitcairn Islands (English colony in the South Pacific): in 1838
- South Australia (under the English Crown): in 1861
- The Isle of Man (British territory): in 1866
- Wyoming Territory (USA): in 1869
- Franceville (South Pacific Island, under Australian influence): in 1879. However, this right was suppressed in 1887, when the French population outnumbered the English 'subjects'.
- New Zealand: in 1893
- Colorado (USA): in 1893
- Utah (USA) and Idaho (USA): in 1893
- All of Australia: in 1902
- Finland (not Anglophone, but Protestant): 1906
- State of Washington (USA): 1910
- California (USA): in 1911
- Kansas (USA), Oregon (USA) and Arizona (USA): in 1912

The next on the list are Norway in 1913, Denmark and Iceland in 1915 and Canada, in 1917 (with the exception of Quebec, Canada's Francophone region, where women would have to wait until 1940).

Then England, that granted limited voting rights to women in 1918 and electoral equality with men in 1928.

In the USA, Women's suffrage would extend to all women in all States the right to vote in 1920, via the 19th Amendment (imposing it upon the French speaking southern states, which continued to resist).

In France, the women would have to wait until 1944...

> *"It wasn't until 1944 that this right was granted to the French women, nearly a century after instituting men's suffrage (1848). And thus, long after India and Turkey.*
>
> *This time-lag is partly explained by the ideological contexts in which this demand was made in France and in the Anglo-Saxon countries. In England and the United States, the suffragettes used both circumstantial and utilitarian arguments based on women's specific contributions to the public collective. ...*
>
> *In France, however, the debate was driven by several, sometimes opposing currents (Universalist and Catholic) and arose from a more philosophical perspective (centered on the advent of the citizen-individual) rather than on a genuinely political one."*
>
> Quotation: Cf. http://gallica.bnf.fr/theme (*suffrage des femmes*), cited 18 November 2007

*******************

With the Fifth Republic (our present governmental constitution), France has experienced several other events in reaction to vertical law and unilateral reasoning. "Mai 68" (May of 1968) is the most vivid example, illustrating the French youth's rebellion against the ever persisting authoritarianism in their country. Their slogan – "Il est interdit d'interdire" (It is forbidden to forbid) – clearly conveyed their objection to the concept of law, as it was being practiced in their country. But this slogan did not get good reception from the public, for its request was unconceivable. Indeed, no social order can subsist in the absence of interdictions (be they simply to prohibit murder). But what the French youth of 68 was truly vindicating was dialogue. They wanted to have their say in the making of their lives. They were complaining that the laws/restrictions were unfair, ineffective and not adapted to the reality they were faced with (all consequences of vertical law). So, although their vindication was badly formulated by their slogan, it expressed a perfectly valid aspiration (calling for cooperation and dialogue). Indeed, for laws/restrictions to be well adjusted, understood and accepted there needs to be cooperation and dialogue. And for an agreement to have any chance of being voluntarily executed (without constraint), it must have been obtained through a bilateral process, through reciprocal engagement—not through unilateral imposition by way of force and blackmail.

> As indicated by the etymology of the word interdiction (inter: between, diction: to speak), an interdiction should be the fruit of an exchange of words. The term explicitly carries within it a bilateral dimension ("between").

# IV. TODAY'S WORLD

## A. FRANCE TODAY

Our country is today in great confusion. Still locked into its hierarchical and centralized power structures—where cooperation and mutual recognition are estranged — it continues to act in accordance to Vertical and Unilateral "law'. **Our country thus adheres to dictatorial logic, while engaging in democratic discourse.**

When overwhelmed with practical problems, the workers at the base of the hierarchal pyramids in the various French institutions (State school system, State-run administrations and nationalized companies) organize strikes and demonstrations to make themselves heard to their "superiors," "up above." But the latter do not to listen... because in the logic of vertical law, taking into account the opinions of "subordinates" is regarded as a sign of weakness (a sign of "fallibility").

France is thus caught between a *democratic discourse* (with its political verbiage of equality and cooperation) and *dictatorial practices* (with its hierarchal structures, based on vertical and unilateral law). Given the profound incompatibility of these two logics, their coexistence creates a profound "malaise."

Here is a short—though not exhaustive—list of the most striking incompatibilities between the two logics:

> ■ In bilateral logic, "to be responsible" means **taking responsibility for one's own actions, choices and projects.**
>
> ■ In unilateral logic, "to be responsible" means being in a position to **hold others accountable** for one's own needs, desires, choices and projects.

- In bilateral logic: freedom of **speech belongs to everyone**.

- In unilateral logic: **only certain "designated" people have a right to speak up**, while others are requested to keep quiet, listen and obey.

---

- In bilateral logic, it is ill-advised to impose oneself upon others (it is not appreciated by the others). The preferred practice is: "*Je propose, tu disposes*" (*I make a suggestion, and you are free to accept/or refuse*).

- In unilateral logic, **imposing oneself is a positive attribute,** because that is how one fulfills one's duty as "*Chef*", "*Responsible*".

But the basic difference (the one that grounds all the others) is:

---

- In bilateral logic: **Law is never personified**; it is never one individual's will. It is a mutually consented agreement made between the concerned parties. One does not have to obey an individual; one has to obey *the law*, which is **a verbalized or written agreement** that can always be revisited.

- In unilateral logic: **Law is personified**. It corresponds to someone's will (a man or woman designated as having "Authority" over others 'below'). His/her word *is the law* and it demands obedience.

---

France navigates between these two logics with difficulty, sometimes complying with the rules of the first, sometimes complying with the rules of the second. Journalists, editorialists and politicians often refer to "schizophrenia of the French people." If schizophrenia there is, it may simply be due to this dichotomy. Indeed, the French have increasingly distanced themselves from the Catholic Church and are gradually freeing themselves from its vertical (top to bottom) logic, with hierarchy that enforces obligation and submission. But this logic is so deeply rooted into the French language and embedded in its institutional structures that it comes as "reflex" in times of crisis. It thus persists, being perpetuated from one generation to the next.

Yes, our country continues to be profoundly Latin. Over and over again, we see political games played out, as governments sacrifice certain key individuals (who serve as "scapegoats") in order to remain in power after having committed errors.

And in regards to certain political offences, we hear strange statements like "Yes, I am responsible, but not guilty." (?)

Moreover, certain "authorities" in psychology or religion—so entrenched in their logic of Unilateral Law—have been heard to affirm that a child must learn to transgress the Law in order to gain maturity/autonomy...! Indeed, if the Law is understood as being Papa's or Mama's will (Latin logic), and that Papa or Mama doesn't let me think or act for myself (i.e. they punish me if I don't fulfill *their* dreams), I will effectively need to confront *my* will against *their will* in order to achieve autonomy and gain in maturity. However, it is <u>certainly not</u> by transgressing the Law—the collectively made agreement contracted by the adults in order to ensure the safety of all—that a youngster will attest to his/her maturity...

## B. AMERICA TODAY

The American example (regarding its structure and institutions) is radically different than the French model. HOWEVER, let it be perfectly clear that I am not presenting the United States of America, *as it is today*, as an archetype of democracy. In the international political scene today, it has turned its back on the essence of what has constituted its foundation. My hope is that in this recollection of History, the Americans will recognize themselves, acknowledge their origins and dare to self-examine their political behavior (so urgently needed).

Many Americans are alarmed by their country's behavior on the international scene in the recent past. America has been led, for the past eight years, by a president who acted not as a "servant and representative of the will of the people," but as *Supreme Will*, like *Magnus*, **He who has Authority over all**. Has he not proclaimed—with disconcerting candor—*"I am the decider"*!? How is it possible that such a statement can be heard from the mouth of the President of the greatest democratic country in the world? From the looks of its foreign policy, as well as its internal workings, President Bush's Administration behaved more like a dictatorship than a democracy: respect for the opinions of those who think differently, the right to self-determination for each and all, the principle of equal voice in the decision making processes, honesty and transparency in its leadership—were all seriously lacking.

Today, America (for its own well-being and that of the whole world) seriously needs to remind itself of its fundamental principles. It needs to recommit itself to respecting free choice and self-determination—for ALL. Despite my belief that the American leaders are correct in thinking that the world's countries would be better off with democratic governments (instead of governments based on dictatorial structures), I do not see how America can *impose* this system onto other countries. Democracy is not something that can be *forced* upon others, because—by definition—imposing "from above" is contrary to democracy. Democracy is *"power to the people, for the people, by the people."* Attempting to *impose* self-determination is absolute nonsense!

By applying power plays in the international scene in the hope of spreading democracy (via the CIA, for example, that "serves as the government's paramilitary hidden hand via covert operations at the direction of the President..."[12]), the United States today intimidates, humiliates and persecutes other peoples on the planet. And it often does so with the use of religious terminology,

---

12      http://en.wikipedia.org/wiki/Central_Intellegence_Agency 7/11/07

which leads to suppose that there is some religious "mission" involved. This is precisely what America's ancestors were fleeing 500 years ago, when they fled from the Catholic persecution in Europe! This striking contradiction leaves many Americans today with a serious malaise. One could write a book entitled "The American Malaise"...

But the truth of the matter is that the United States is no longer a fully democratic country. Significant changes have occurred over the last decades in the American political landscape that enables the modern federal government to behave today as "All Powerful". <u>A significant increase in presidential powers</u> (regarding foreign affairs) and in federal power (regarding internal affairs) has taken place since World War II that has distanced America from its initial concept of democracy. The original political structures instituted by the American founding fathers (initially intended to promote liberty and justice for all) were specifically constituted to protect the individual citizens from abuse of power hungry "authorities."

Much can be said about the increasing presidential powers in the USA and how it has distanced America from its democratic origins. But that is not the subject of this book. Here, I am writing *about* France and *for* France. And I am doing so because I am French born, and also because I believe that *examination begins at home*. I dare to hope that this initiative of mine (helping my country diagnose its malaise in order to help seek remedies) will invite others—of other cultures—to do the same for their respective countries. And I hope that my description of the origins of American democracy will ring "true" to the ears of my American readers, offering them an "outside perspective" in order to better see their own malaise.

I would really like to see America protect what she has that is most unique and most precious, namely: its principle of *"Liberty and justice for all"* and *All equal under the law.* It is thanks to this concept of equal opportunity—structurally inscribed in its institutions—that the Democratic Republic of the United States has been a refuge for so many immigrants throughout the world. Its structures have enabled its population to evolve over time, slowly rehabilitating individuals from around the world that were elsewhere treated as "inferior" and "inept."

To prevent my analysis from being used to further feed religious battles, that have already caused so much damage, I must emphasize the following point: the fact that the Protestant movement historically and actively contributed to the development of democracy does not make the Protestants "closer to God" than other people. Nor does it give them the right to claim any exclusive privilege.

What led the first Protestants to create this democratic political system was their very pronounced aversion to the abuse of power, abuses for which they had already paid a great price. The Bible, which directly addresses the issue of slavery, supported their fight against abuse (as it did for the Jewish people, enslaved in Egypt, and for Black people, enslaved in America). All oppressed people around the world could use the Bible to support their social and/or religious oppression (and many have). But the Bible does not hold the monopoly to this effect...

The second characteristic that advantaged the Protestant pilgrims of the "New World" was their cultural diversity. They came from various European countries, speaking different languages and practicing different customs. They were bound by the singular conviction that they were **all equal** (all brothers, with one and the same Father). This is why they created political structures where a person—independent of his cultural origin—was allowed to express himself with an "equal voice." This too could be extended to other peoples/countries.

If the Protestants were to consider themselves "intrinsically superior/closer to God than the others" for having actively contributed to the creation of the first religious and political democratic structures, they would face the risk of becoming persecutors themselves. For it is precisely when one believes to be "superior" to others that one begins to think of oneself as "exceptional" (i.e. "above the ordinary, common man") and thus "*more* deserving" (which leads to the exclusion of those considered "inferior" and "*less* deserving").

## C. PROTESTANTS TODAY

In regards to the Protestants today, I am very sad (and quite worried) to see the number of churches stemming from the Reformation that are today ignorant of their origin and that have cut themselves from their roots. Some have unknowingly deprived themselves of their basic treasure: the principle of equality in respect and consideration, the notion of "all equal under God." Just like the Catholic Church against which they protested 500 years ago, these churches (many whom still call themselves Protestant) have adopted a form of structural hierarchy, placing one individual "at the top" (almost always of masculine gender) that they call "clergyman"—pastor or guru— and that they qualify as "closer to God". Many of these men pretend that they know *who* God is, *what* He says and *what* He wants. Thus, they speak "in the name of God", and are followed by pious parishioners who listen to them "religiously," without questioning. These religious "authorities" drill their "truths" into their followers (who drink up their words as if they came from God Himself) and take advantage of the fascination they evoke by threatening those who fail to conform to their demands. This phenomenon – by product of idolatry (a phenomenon strongly reprimanded in Biblical texts...paradoxical, isn't it?) – is rife with many serious consequences. It throws followers back into the troublesome waters of submission, where individual free-will and freedom of choice is trampled by the obligation to obey the orders of a few individuals (who pose as their "authorities," claiming to know *better* than they what is good for them). And, it is in the name of their supposedly loving and merciful God that these religious authorities punish (condemn, shun, humiliate, ostracize, etc.) those who don't follow in their path. Dangerous regressions in women's and children's rights take place in these religious contexts. The democratic principle of "all equal in voice and consideration", being dismissed, leaves room, once again, for abuse and discrimination.

# CONCLUSION

Two opposing logics are at work today in the France:

- One is based on a vertical concept of LAW, where laws are legislated by the imposition of one's will over all the others, and where "authority" is obtained by force/ intimidation and sustained by power plays.

- The other is based on a horizontal, bilateral concept of LAW, where laws are legislated by mutual agreement of all parties involved and "authority" is obtained by competence and sustained by cooperation, trust and honesty.

The first is DICTATORIAL (with a few individuals *dictating* their will upon all the others) and is the logic around which our country is structured. The second is DEMOCRATIC, striving for equal opportunity for all. These two logics are *incompatible*.

France is a country of dictatorial structures with democratic pretense. This dichotomy causes a national malaise, creating political tensions, social unrest, and much interpersonal violence. It is time that we look at this problem and deal with it head on. The health of our citizens and of our country depends on it.

# PART THREE: *REMEDY*

## I. <u>DEMOCRACY – Antithesis to Vertical Law</u>

The Latin concept of authority—the one that restricts the right to think-and-decide to only a designated few—is the underlying cause of injustice in France (and in probably in all the other Latin countries). In this dictatorial system, where social order is held by "the will of a few" endowed with the power to command all the others (forcing them to obey), manipulative strategies –such as discounting, threatening and intimidating– are legitimated and encouraged. Vertical and Unilateral Law, operating at every level of our institutions (pyramidal hierarchal structures with highly centralized power), permeates every sphere of our lives, inviting the presence of power plays, violence and abuse.

DEMOCRACY is the antithesis to dictatorship (Vertical Law). It is an officially structured system that provides cooperation, honesty and transparency. It does so by guaranteeing the freedom of speech (to all and on all subjects) and by granting a voice for all (adults) in the decision-making processes. This institutionalized practice – that aims to give equal opportunity to all – has the great advantage of protecting its individual members from coercive behavior. It dismantles "hierarchies" and encourages competency amongst those holding positions of leadership. By mandating dialogue (institutionalizing "spaces" for discussion and questioning), it obliges the leaders to be cautious of the way they use their power (since they will be held accountable for their acts).

Of course, there will always be those who disregard others, believing themselves "more deserving" than others. This is because there will always be religions to preach the idea that some humans are "more deserving" of consideration than others. According to these religions, God grants love and consideration only to those who "deserve it"; He will not grant it freely, *to all*. Though the criteria of who deserves consideration will vary from one religion to another, the bottom line is always that only the individuals who fit *their criteria* of "deserving" will get the love, attention and consideration they need.

In some religions the criteria for "deserving consideration" are birth attributes: gender (men), family blood (aristocracy), and economic status (land owners). In other religions, they are more personal attributes (one's intelligence, accomplishments, diplomas and/or profession).

Whatever the criteria put forward by the religious leaders, the people are led to believe that only the individuals who fit those specific criteria deserve consideration. And consequently, those who *do not* fit them *do not* deserve consideration, i.e. *deserve to die* (and *will* die, because deprived of social consideration, no one can survive).

Yes, there will always be those who think themselves "Superior beings" for meeting the *set prerequisites*. And they will enforce *that* set of prerequisites onto others, looking down upon the individuals who do not comply. They will act as if They-Know-Best about what others should do with their lives, and they will be quick to judge and quick to condemn. They will ostracize those who prove them wrong and will discredit the person who achieves what they so eagerly strive to achieve.

We will never eliminate this phenomenon. But we can stop legitimizing and institutionalizing it!

By abandoning our unilateral concept of Law and replacing it with the democratic practices of mutually accepted agreements, we will give everyone the opportunity to get what they need, to feel good about themselves, and to take their life into their own hands. By granting the FREEDOM OF SPEECH to all, we will free the access (for all) to the various sources of power and satisfaction. *That* is the great FREEDOM that democracy provides.

This, however, requires a structural modification of all our institutions (familial, social, political and religious). And these changes must begin *at home, in our families,* where our most intimate needs are to be met. To assure that everyone's needs are met, the various adult members of the household must share equal voice in the decision-making process, and the children must feel free to speak up and be heard, *with equal consideration granted to each sibling.* Even though a child's voice cannot weigh that of an adult in the decision-making process, it is absolutely necessary for children to feel free to speak up. They need to express their needs and their feelings. This does not mean that they must get their way (because children don't know what is good or bad for them - they need parental guidance for that). But if there is no dialogue between the children and the parents, there is no way that the parents can know what is actually going on in their children's lives. And without that knowledge, a parent cannot provide adjusted care to their child.

## II.  __FREEDOM__

Beyond these necessary <u>structural modifications,</u> that would offer freedom of speech to all (which is the basis of democracy), a few concepts need to be redefined, in order to free us from the discriminatory logic of Vertical Law:

### A.  FREE FROM LEGITIMIZED BULLYING

We need to abandon the Latin concept of *authority* and have our chefs manage <u>projects, not people</u>.  We need clear job descriptions that call for specific tasks and specific technical capacities, so that we are hired not to serve our bosses, but to serve projects.  Let's make it very clear to all that people are not objects to be owned.  Owners own <u>things, not people</u> (have you ever noticed how some people guard a relationship as if they were "guarding their territory"? They decide who approaches that person and what that person can do/not do, accept/not accept say/not say...).

### B.  FREE TO SERVE FREELY

Everyone needs to serve <u>a purpose</u>.  But no one should be subjected to (nor subject themselves to) serving <u>a person</u> (in the sense of servitude). We don't serve someone; we <u>offer services</u> to someone. The difference is subtle, but it is of extreme pertinence. It's the difference between voluntary service and servitude (service by obligation). It's a question of respecting the individual's FREE WILL to serve (and not be forced into service by some coercive manner).  The fundamental question is: Who is the master of my actions and of my thought process in the course of my service?  If we want our nation to be formed of free-willing, considerate and responsible citizens, we, ourselves, need to be free-willing, considerate and responsible citizens (meaning "in charge of" and "held accountable for" our own actions, in regards to others). And we need to request that from others, and <u>help our children grow in that direction.</u>

### C. FREE TO REAP ONE'S OWN HARVEST

Let's truly believe that everyone has something unique and specific to offer to our society. Based on that premise, let's give everyone an equal chance to do so. Let's let everyone speak for him/herself and choose his/her own direction in life. Let's respect the fact that everyone has a mind of their own and can use it, if given the chance. Let's stop thinking for others or presume that we know better than them what they should do with their lives. Let's let everyone make personal initiatives and take credit for their own achievements (free of reprisal from an individual that might feel offended for having been "surpassed" by a smart initiative).

Let's let *everyone* reap the harvest of their *own* efforts, and put the recognition back where it belongs!

### D. FREE OUR HUMAN RESOURCES AND LIBERATE OUR ENERGIES

The vast majority of the French people would benefit from abandoning the Latin concept of authority. Freed of the stress of having to serve someone else's dreams and fight someone else's personal battles (resulting from their own frustrations of having been "pushed around"), we could put our energy to positive, constructive use. We could serve in ways that best suit us and in which we are most competent. The fact is that we waste *so much* energy in trying to stay safe under the "chef's baguette" (conducting stick), that if we were freed of it (the chef's baguette), we'd find ourselves with so much more energy to spare - energy that could serve a more constructive purpose. Our country's economy would find itself greatly revitalized by this subsequent deployment of life forces, and in the end, we would all be happier, stronger and more powerful.

## E.  FREE THE WORLD OF OUR POWER PLAYS

And as a nation, we could use this gained power to productive purposes; not to threaten other less powerful countries.  For we will have understood that "bullying" others (power playing) does not build trust, but on the contrary, aggravates tensions.  Moreover, our newly gained strength may serve as a model of persuasion for other countries to lean in the same direction, encouraging them to adopt the democratic logic. And then, perhaps, our better understanding of the benefits of democracy will help us see the necessity of forming an international democratic structure to prevent "power plays" between nations and deal intelligently with international issues *(granting equal respect and consideration for all)*.


We would then experience the immense pride of having fulfilled our popular adage:


## *"France, pays de la liberté!"*
(France, country of freedom!)

"Don't walk behind me; I may not want to lead.
Don't walk before me; I may not want to follow.
Walk by my side and let's be friends."

Albert Camus

## TEXTS that lead to the Declaration of Human Rights [13]

1.  The **Magna Carta** (1215) in England: Charter drafted by English exiles in France in revolt against their King, John "Lackland."

2.  The **Bill of Rights** (1628) in England: Demand for political power simultaneously guaranteeing the rights and liberties of individuals (protection of the right to innocence, freedom of movement, etc.).

3.  **Habeas Corpus** (1679) in England: formalized the Petition of 1628 (a law to better guarantee the freedom of subjects).

4.  The **Bill of Rights** (1689): definition of the rights of Parliament and citizens.

5.  The **Virginia Bill of Rights** (May 1779) in America: took into consideration the ideas of political philosopher John Locke, who deemed that there could only be separation between Church and State.

6.  The **Declaration of Independence** (July 1776) in the United States: In essence, it is a revival of the Virginia Bill of Rights, which declares "we hold these truths to be self-evident, that all men are created equal, that they are endowed by their Creator with certain unalienable Rights, that among these are Life, Liberty and the pursuit of Happiness" and "that to secure these rights, Governments are instituted among Men."

---

[13]    As cited in the Foreword of *Les Droits de l'Homme*, éditions Librio, 1998

7. The **Declaration of the Rights of Man and of the Citizen** (1789) in France: A declaration of the principle that was inspired by the American document of 1776, but which, due to its broad scope, is addressed to men throughout time and in all countries, hence consecrating its "universal" vocation.

*******************

The **Universal Declaration of Human Rights** (1948) was proclaimed by the United Nations General Assembly. This document was solemnly passed in Paris on 10 December 1948 by a vote of 48 in favor out of 56, with 8 countries abstaining (these included the USSR and 5 Soviet Bloc countries, South Africa and Saudi Arabia.

# BIBLIOGRAPHY

1. *The Other Side of Power*, by Claude Steiner, Grove Press, 1981
2. *Achieving Emotional Literacy,* by Claude Steiner, William Morrow, 1997
3. *Scripts People Live: Transactional Analysis of Life Scripts*, by Claude Steiner, Grove Press, 1994
4. *A Warm Fuzzy Tale*, by Claude Steiner, Jalmar Press, 1983
5. *Games People Play*, by Eric Berne, Stock, 1967
6. *Emotional Intelligence: Why It Can Matter More Than IQ*, by Daniel Goleman, Bantam, 1997
7. *How Real Is Real?: Confusion, Disinformation, Communication*, by Paul Watzlawick, Random House, 1976
8. *Don't think of an Elephant*, by George Lakoff, Scribe Publications, 2005
9. *La nouvelle grille*, by Henri Laborit, Robert Laffont, 1974
10. *Eloge de la fuite*, by Henri Laborit, Robert Laffont, 1976
11. *Le Sentiment Religieux Primitif*, first course in the series *L'Histoire des Religions*, by Gilbert Carayon
12. *La Subversion du Christianisme*, by Jacques Ellul, édition le Seuil, 1984
13. *La Bible et sa culture*, under the direction of Michel Quesnel and Philippe Gruson, Desclée de Brouwer, 2000
14. *La Réforme*, by Richard Stauffer, Que sais-je ? PUF
15. *Les Réformes*, by Olivier Christin, éditions Découvertes Gallimard
16. *Le Sacrifice interdit (Freud et la Bible)*, by Marie Balmary, éd. Grasset, 1986
17. *Les Droits de l'Homme*, éditions Librio, 1998
18. *Le Petit Robert, volumes 1 and 2*, (dictionary of the French language),1996 edition
19. *Etymologies du français*, by René Garrus, éditons Belin, 1996
20. *Dictionnaire étymologique et historique du français*, Larousse, (1993 version)

21. *Dictionnaire illustré de l'Histoire de France*, Alain Decaux of the French Academy and André Castelot, éd. Perrin
22. *Encyclopédie Générale Larousse*, Vol. 1, Librairie Larousse, 1967
23. *Quid 98*, Editions Robert Laffont, 1997
24. *Atlas de la Philosophie*, by Kunzmann, Burkard and Wiedmann, éd. Livre de Poche. Encyclopédies d'aujourd'hui.
25. *Les plus belles pages manuscrites de l'histoire de France*, National Library, éd. Robert Laffont
26. *National Geographic Atlas of World History*, 1997
27. The World Almanac (and Book of Facts) 2005, World Almanac Books, USA
28. Time Almanac 2005, Pearson Education, 2005
29. Wikipedia Encyclopedia on Internet: http://fr.wikipedia and http://en.wikipedia
30. *Napoleon, Petit guide*, AEDIS, édition 03200, Vichy

www.ingramcontent.com/pod-product-compliance
Lightning Source LLC
Chambersburg PA
CBHW072330290526
45794CB00002B/820